Praise for *Brilliant Strategy for Business*

'*Brilliant Strategy for Business* is brilliant! This comprehensive strategy primer deserves to be read by managers and strategists everywhere.'

Dr Bruce Ahlstrand, Co-Author of Strategy Safari: Your Complete Guide Through the Wilds of Strategic Management *and Professor of Strategic Management at Trent University, Ontario, Canada*

'A great management book which combines strategy, change management, personal development and system-thinking aspects. It's unique in its kind compared to other strategy books.'

Zoltan Czegledy, Global Commodity Manager, Strategic Procurement, Bombardier

'*Brilliant Strategy for Business* hits the mark at two levels. Firstly, it provides a great, easy-to-understand synopsis of the major tools and approaches used in developing effective business strategy. Secondly, and perhaps more importantly, it doesn't just look at traditional approaches but challenges the reader to consider how strategy will be developed and deployed in today's paradigm-shifting business environment with its mega trends, global economic influences, and rapidly changing generational and consumer driven change.

Whether you are new to strategic planning and looking for an easy entry point into the ideas and language, or a more seasoned leader who needs a refresher, this book will definitely give you ideas, challenges and knowledge presented in an easy-to-consume manner.'

Paul Major, Director, Strategic Delivery and Change

brilliant

strategy for business

PEARSON

At Pearson, we believe in learning – all kinds of learning for all kinds of people. Whether it's at home, in the classroom or in the workplace, learning is the key to improving our life chances.

That's why we're working with leading authors to bring you the latest thinking and best practices, so you can get better at the things that are important to you. You can learn on the page or on the move, and with content that's always crafted to help you understand quickly and apply what you've learned.

If you want to upgrade your personal skills or accelerate your career, become a more effective leader or more powerful communicator, discover new opportunities or simply find more inspiration, we can help you make progress in your work and life.

Pearson is the world's leading learning company. Our portfolio includes the Financial Times and our education business, Pearson International.

Every day our work helps learning flourish, and wherever learning flourishes, so do people.

To learn more, please visit us at **www.pearson.com/uk**

brilliant

strategy for business

How to plan, implement and evaluate strategy at
any level of management

Chris Dalton

PEARSON

Harlow, England • London • New York • Boston • San Francisco • Toronto • Sydney • Auckland • Singapore • Hong Kong
Tokyo • Seoul • Taipei • New Delhi • Cape Town • São Paulo • Mexico City • Madrid • Amsterdam • Munich • Paris • Milan

PEARSON EDUCATION LIMITED
Edinburgh Gate
Harlow CM20 2JE
United Kingdom
Tel: +44 (0)1279 623623
Web: www.pearson.com/uk

First published 2016 (print and electronic)

© Dalton Training Limited 2016 (print and electronic)

ISBN: 978-1-292-10784-4 (print)
 978-1-292-10786-8 (PDF)
 978-1-292-10787-5 (ePub)

British Library Cataloguing-in-Publication Data
A catalogue record for the print edition is available from the British Library

Library of Congress Cataloging-in-Publication Data
Names: Dalton, Chris, author.
Title: Brilliant strategy for business : how to plan, implement and evaluate strategy at any level of management / Chris Dalton.
Description: Harlow, England ; New York : Pearson, 2016. | Includes bibliographical references and index.
Identifiers: LCCN 2015044283 (print) | LCCN 2015048195 (ebook) | ISBN 9781292107844 | ISBN 9781292107868 () | ISBN 9781292107875 ()
Subjects: LCSH: Strategic planning. | Management.
Classification: LCC HD30.28 .D35 2016 (print) | LCC HD30.28 (ebook) | DDC 658.4/012--dc23
LC record available at http://lccn.loc.gov/2015044283

10 9 8 7 6 5 4 3 2 1
20 19 18 17 16

Series design by David Carroll & Co

Print edition typeset in 10/14pt Plantin MT Pro by SPi Global
Print edition printed in Great Britain by Henry Ling Ltd, at the Dorset Press, Dorchester, Dorset

NOTE THAT ANY PAGE CROSS REFERENCES REFER TO THE PRINT EDITION

Contents

About the author

A dynamic and creative tutor and facilitator, **Chris Dalton** is Associate Professor of Management Learning at Henley Business School at the University of Reading in the UK. He joined Henley in November 2005 and until 2010 was the Director of the Henley MBA (Flexible Learning), a programme with over 3,000 executives worldwide. Since 2010 he has taught and facilitated the Personal Development module on the MBA. His research interests centre on reflective practice in management and leadership.

Chris has accumulated 25 years of experience in management education and training in the UK and abroad. Before Henley he worked at the CEU Business School in Budapest, Hungary as MBA Program Director and has run corporate workshops and seminars related to management development in many parts of the world, including South Africa, Central Europe and the Middle East.

Chris holds a PhD in Management Learning and Leadership from Lancaster University and an MBA from Henley. A Fellow of the Higher Education Academy he is a visiting Professor of Management at COTRUGLI Business School in Croatia. His first book, *The Every Day MBA*, was published by Pearson in January 2015.

Acknowledgements

No one learns as much about a subject as one who is forced to teach it.

Peter F. Drucker

Drucker was correct that teaching acquaints you more with a topic than listening about it does. What he did not say was that it is only when you write about a subject that your acquaintance really becomes intimate.

Although this book has been a personal project, produced mostly in isolation, it would not have been possible – or much good – without the support and feedback of those around me. I am grateful to my wife, Gina, for the love and patience that tolerated the writing space. I would also like to thank Professors Marc Day and Jane McKenzie at Henley Business School, and Cigdem Gogus, Rupa Datta, Clive Randall and Sabine Jones for their time and generous comments on drafts at various stages. Finally, a thank you to Steve Temblett, my editor at Pearson – not least for sharing my taste in music.

Publisher's acknowledgements

We are grateful to the following for permission to reproduce copyright material:

Figures
Figure 3.2 from 'Strategies for diversification', *Harvard Business Review* 35(5), September–October, pp. 113–124 (Ansoff, I. 1957).

Reprinted by permission of *Harvard Business Review*. Copyright © 1957 by the Harvard Business School Publishing Corporation, all rights reserved; Figure 4.2 from *Competitive Advantage, The Free Press* (Porter, M.E. 2004). Reprinted with the permission of The Free Press, a Division of Simon & Schuster, Inc., from COMPETITIVE ADVANTAGE: CREATING AND SUSTAINING SUPERIOR PERFORMANCE by Michael E. Porter. Copyright © 1985 by Michael E. Porter. All rights reserved; Figure 5.1 from *Strategy Safari: Your Complete Guide Through the Wilds of Strategic Management*. 2nd Ed. (Mintzberg, H., Ahlstrand, B. and Lampel, J. 2008). Reproduced with permission of Pearson Education Limited, © Henry Mintzberg, Bruce Ahlstrand and Joseph Lampel 1998, 2009; Figure 7.2 adapted from *Resolving Social Conflicts, and Field Theory in Social Science*, American Psychology Association (Lewin, K. 1997), p. 313. Copyright © 1997 by the American Psychological Association. Adapted with permission. The use of APA information does not imply endorsement by APA; Figure 7.3 from http://www.kotterinternational.com/our-principles/changesteps/changesteps, Kotter International; Figure 7.4 from 'Toward a theory of stakeholder identification and salience: Defining the principle of who and what really counts', *The Academy of Management Review* 22(4), pp. 853–886 (Mitchell, R., Agle, B. and Wood, D. 1997). Copyright © 1997 by ACADEMY OF MANAGEMENT. Reprinted with permission via Copyright Clearance Center; Figure 7.5 from 'Using the balanced scorecard as a strategic management system', *Harvard Business Review* 74(1), January–February, pp. 75–85 (Kaplan, R.S. and Norton, D.P. 1996). Reprinted by permission of *Harvard Business Review*. Copyright © 1996 by the Harvard Business School Publishing Corporation, all rights reserved; Figure 7.7 from 'A leader's framework for decision making', *Harvard Business Review* 85(11), November, pp. 69–76 (Snowden D.J. and Boone M.E. 2007). Reprinted by permission of *Harvard Business Review*. Copyright © 2007 by the Harvard Business School Publishing

Corporation, all rights reserved; Figure 9.2 adapted from Price-waterhouseCoopers 2015 survey, 'The hidden talent: Ten ways to identify and retain transformational leaders'.

Tables

Table 2.1 from 'Evolution and revolution as enterprises grow', *Harvard Business Review* 50(4), July–August, pp. 37–46 (Greiner, L.E. 1972). Reprinted by permission of *Harvard Business Review*. Copyright © 1972 by the Harvard Business School Publishing Corporation, all rights reserved; Table 7.1 from *A Manager's Guide to Leadership: An Action Learning Approach*. 2nd Ed. McGraw-Hill (Pedler, M., Burgoyne, J. and Boydell, T. 2010), pp. 107–108. © 2010, reproduced with kind permission of McGraw-Hill Education. All Rights Reserved.

Text

Text on page 176 from http://www.nhsconfed.org/resources/key-statistics-on-the-nhs. Reproduced with permission of Clare-Lyons Collins; Text on page 232 from http://www.interfaceglobal.com/company/mission-vision.aspx. Reproduced with permission of Interface Inc.; Text on pages 234–236 adapted from John Whittington using material from Whittington, J. (2016) *Systemic Coaching and Constellations*. 2nd Ed. London: Kogan Page. Reproduced with permission of John Whittington; Text on page 244 from *Tao Te Ching: A New English Version* (Mitchell, S. 2006), p. 1 and Verse 17. Excerpts from TAO TE CHING BY LAO TZU, WITH FORWARD NOTES, by STEPHEN MITCHELL. Translation copyright © 1988 by Stephen Mitchell. Reprinted by permission of Harper Collins Publishers; Interview on pages 250–251 from Heather Couper, Straight from the Cow. Reproduced with permission of Heather Couper.

Introduction

We see the world not as it is, but as we are.

Anthony De Mello

As one of the most popular subjects in management and business, there have been many books written about strategy . . . and here is another one. So, why this book? Who is it for? What is it trying to achieve? How can you apply what it says to ensure your own success?

These are great questions for a strategist to ask.

Strategy is finding out *why* your business is here, what it stands for, who it is for and *what* it aims to achieve next. It is about identifying what sets your organisation apart, and about the actions you will take to make sure it achieves its purpose now and into the future.

Before you read any further, take a look at the list overleaf. Each statement reflects a possible approach to strategy. Which comes nearest to your current understanding? Which most challenges it?

'Strategy is the boss's job, not mine.'	• Owned by the visionaries at the top or by a few entrepreneurial senior managers, strategy is driven by them and is not my responsibility.
'Strategy is designing a policy and then sticking to a plan.'	• Process driven, with detailed scenarios carefully worked out by specialists or experts. Often contained in a document, our strategy is 'written in stone'.
'Strategy follows an analysis of our competitive position.'	• Strategy results from balancing a careful analysis of the external industry environment with our internal resources. It's about winning, again and again.
'Strategy is learning from what's happening all around.'	• Our strategy unfolds as we go, and is only clear to us when we look back. Strategy is learning by doing, and we trust that process. It's our story and it defines us.
'Strategy is ecology.'	• Not a question of winning or losing, strategy is being in tune with the natural ebb and flow of the whole environment. We don't survive without our environment.

Each could be an answer to the question of what strategy is, and each reflects a different school of thought explored in this book. We can, however, dismiss the first on the list here and now. Top management teams are certainly involved in strategy, but the process also involves the whole organisation. You included. Strategy is concerned with what needs to be done to ensure the survival of the organisation, which means you already have a vested interest.

brilliant tip

Whether you are a corporate CEO, a business unit leader or a functional manager – *you are a strategist.*

What *kind* of strategist you are depends on two things. First, your position in your organisation and, second, which of the schools you decide is closest to your own.

Do not be put off by the news that there is not one universally accepted definition of the word strategy, or that the subject feels a bit messy (though it is certainly true that the language of strategic thinking can sometimes seem technical and confusing). Avoiding too much jargon, *Brilliant Strategy for Business* will show you how to find ways to think about, implement and evaluate strategy and how to see that all the day-to-day activities of management have a strategic function and meaning. Being a brilliant business strategist will call for alertness and for ways of seeing what others take for granted, so the most important step in your development as a strategist will be your self-awareness. This book will encourage you to ask the right questions to set you on a course of change as a manager.

 **example**

Coca-Cola bottlers in Hungary

In the mid-1990s I took a group of British Executive MBA students on a study tour to Hungary. This included a site visit to a brand new and state-of-the-art Coca-Cola bottling facility, outside Budapest. The Hungarian economy had recently emerged from four decades of communist rule and had undergone volatile transformation. In this new era and in this relatively small market, the world's two largest soft-drinks companies, Pepsico and Coca-Cola, had engaged in no-holds-barred, head-to-head competition for market share. The competition was an intense roller-coaster ride.

We sat in the boardroom at the plant and were invited to sample the product, before being greeted by the CEO, a softly spoken Australian. 'I'm going to tell you about our strategy here in Hungary', he said and then added, 'what it is this week, anyway.' He was not being flippant. At the corporate level, Coca-Cola's strategy can move at the rate of syrup, but at the business level it was flowing rapidly amongst complex relationships with suppliers, retailers, customers and rivals. Down at the functional level, we learnt, it was often 'all hands to the pumps' to deal with the day-to-day surprises inherent in an emerging economy and with a competitor that had invested heavily in its own strategy to beat you.

The Coca-Cola executive knew that strategy is multi-faceted, complex and purposeful. Every organisation in the world has purpose. Purpose consists of three elements:

1 Why the organisation is here.

2 What circumstances, people and culture are in place to sustain it now.

3 How the desire for continued existence into the future is translated into action.

Together, the why, what and how of strategy create a direction, a story or trajectory that defines what the organisation is.

 **brilliant** tip

Strategy is an idea. Nothing is more powerful than an idea.

Brilliant Strategy for Business features:

● **Fast learning:** the most important concepts and theories are explained using concise and plain language.

● **Brilliant real-world examples:** illustrations taken from practice show how managers and organisations scan the business environment, how they ask the right questions and how they implement that information.

● **Brilliant tips:** packed with practical ideas and challenging *questions* for you to action in your day-to-day work, regardless of where you are in your career.

How the book is organised

Brilliant Strategy for Business will build your confidence to make everyday choices into strategic ones. The book is in three parts.

- **Part 1: Getting to grips with strategy** (Chapters 1 to 3) starts with a short history of the concept and then explores corporate strategy, which is how organisations see the big issues of the wider relationship between them and their environment, how they decide where they want to go and how they resource the changes that happen along the way. The world of strategic design and planning often feels remote from what managers spend their time *actually* doing, so this first section will help you prepare to get the most out of the rest of the book. It is essential to understand what keeps senior management awake at night, in order to appreciate how every part of the organisation can make a contribution to success.

- **Part 2: Business level strategy** (Chapters 4 to 7) is about where change actually happens, in implementation. In fact, most of us work at this level and we encounter strategy via the consequences of the decisions made at a corporate level. You will discover how the day-to-day management of resources has a strategic connection and how mastery of different business functions can contribute to strategic outcomes.

- **Part 3: Strategic thinking in a changing world** (Chapters 8 and 9) looks at the direction strategy is taking today. Purpose-led transformation, values-based leadership and corporate social responsibility, for example, are hot topics amongst the world's leading business experts at the moment. I end with how I see strategic thinking – through holistic and systemic eyes. Along the way, I have inserted plenty of real-life illustrations, each of which paints a picture for you to interpret. After the epilogue, I have included some short biographical sketches of some key movers and shakers, as well as suggestions for a little further reading and thinking.

Strategy expert Henry Mintzberg and his co-authors begin their entertaining book *Strategy Safari* with an Indian folk tale.[1] Six blind men are placed in front of an elephant and each is asked to describe it. Of course, each touches a different part of the animal and concludes that the remainder must be the same. Before we begin, I want you to acknowledge that you, too, infer every new situation from a fixed point of view. You filter life through your prejudices, biases, attachments to past experiences and beliefs about how the world is. That worldview is essential for you to make sense and operate effectively in the day-to-day and, when things are going normally, you rarely need to question it. But, as soon as something out of the ordinary happens, or when you want to learn something new, all the shortcuts and thinking habits get in the way. Just when you need to be creative, you have less freedom and fewer choices available to you; exactly the opposite of what you need to be a brilliant strategist.

There are two drivers to learning and change. The first is *boredom*. Do not underrate this – nothing makes change look more interesting than having nothing to do. The second is *curiosity*. Boredom and curiosity are the push and pull keys to self-development. And self-development is the only worthwhile route to becoming a brilliant strategist.

I hope you enjoy exploring.

References

[1] Mintzberg, H., Ahlstrand, B. and Lampel, J. (2008) *Strategy Safari: Your Complete Guide Through the Wilds of Strategic Management.* 2nd Ed. Harlow: FT Prentice Hall.

PART 1

Getting to grips with strategy

If you don't know where you are going, any road will take you there.

Lewis Carroll, *Alice in Wonderland*

Are you the type who is happy to go through life leaving things to chance? All of us can afford to do this some of the time but if you are a manager in an organisation – especially if you are the person in charge – almost certainly, this will not be your instinct. Most managers I meet are interested in control. You may feel a sense of responsibility for others, such as your customers, the people who work for you and your suppliers but, when you are responsible for making sure that investors or founders get a reasonable return on their investment, you want to be as in control of your destiny as possible. Above everything else, a manager's job is to be concerned with **value creation,** and this is a strong motivation to impose control.

brilliant definition

Value creation

This is what your organisation exists to do. It will aim to create value by solving fundamental problems faced by its customers (profitably).

The *way* you go about your business today is called your **business model.**

Business model

This is the system that is in place to create and capture value. It is both your description of your system and the system itself. If these are in harmony, then all is well. If not, watch out!

Every organisation has a business model, even if it has a bad, hidden or chaotic one, and its purpose is to capture value in net profits, surpluses and dividends. Strategy is another word for the delicate relationship between you and your environment as you attempt to manage and control all the resources at your disposal. Established firms have business models that are the result of planning, learning and random chance over time.

The word *change* is never far from your lips when you are a strategist, but you will not always have it your own way. Complete control will, inevitably, evade you, but that does not mean you have to let everything slip through your fingers. You can get a grip on strategy, but you face three limitations:

1 Many important *external* factors are not in your direct control.

2 There is usually a limited supply of the *internal* resources you need to create and capture value. Scarcity usually means you have to make tough choices (and over-supply of unwanted or out-of-date resources can also stop you being agile).

3 There is a tension between your wish to act and the ethical obligations or responsibilities imposed by the law or societal norms. There may also be a tension between what *you* think is best and what those above you in your organisation want you to do.

Strategy means finding and keeping a direction – a sense of purpose – by balancing these elements in such a way that the whole organisation prospers. It is, by definition, dynamic. If you have a multi-business, multi-industry or multi-division organisation, then this is called **corporate strategy.** In this part of the book, I want to explore what we usually mean when we talk about strategy – and what it means to call yourself a strategist. This is the big picture – how managers go about defining their businesses and how they make sense of their external environment to continue whatever the mission is.

brilliant question

Before you read on, spend a few minutes considering what in *your* organisation defines success. What sorts of things tell you that you are on the right track?

In tough economic times or in a crisis, it may feel like success is simply to be still in one piece at the end of your planning period. In stormy seas, it may be that the only strategy is all hands on deck! But most of the time in management the key to success is whether you *produce a net level of economic return* (i.e. a profit, or a surplus) *from now into the future*. If there is one thing that drives corporate strategy, then it is that goal.

However, before tackling the organisation I would like to start with the most important component in the strategic mix – you.

CHAPTER 1

How to be a brilliant business strategist

Some people believe football is a matter of life and death. I am very disappointed with that attitude. I can assure you it is much, much more important than that.

Bill Shankly, legendary manager of Liverpool FC

How this chapter will help you

Where are we going? What is our plan to get there? Many have concluded that this is what strategy is about. This chapter tells you where the rest of book is going and how it plans to get there. We start to define strategy (though it is better not to jump to conclusions) and see how holding on to past success can sometimes create problems. The keys to being a good strategist are (i) passion, (ii) good judgement and (iii) a mindset of curiosity and exploration.

Introduction

There is no doubt that strategy matters. To be a brilliant business strategist you need to have straight in your mind three things:

1 What strategy is and why it matters.
2 How to act to achieve strategic goals.
3 Who you are as a strategic leader.

One sure sign of mastery of management is that you see beyond the operational and the day-to-day. As you gain more responsibility in your career, the underlying purpose of the organisation starts to be a much more important factor in your decision making. Whatever your management level, you must learn how to communicate your vision of what needs to be done. This is true regardless of whether you are the CEO at the top, a functional head or an operational manager lower down.

I want you to have plenty of takeaways from reading this book. A lot of strategy is about what happens in implementation (*what*), but every strategist knows that implementation usually follows some kind of formulation (*how*), which flows from a purpose (*why*). For this reason, we cannot jump straight to action – we must begin our journey by defining our terms.

 **brilliant** tip

> When defining strategy, do not be in a rush to reach firm conclusions. As you travel, be an explorer who sees things as if for the first time.

What strategy is

Professors of strategy in business schools often use a metaphor – victory – to introduce strategy as a concept. Echoes of war and politics abound, with reference to Sun Tzu's *The Art of War*, ancient Greek sea battles, Nelson's tactics at the Battle of Trafalgar or Machiavelli's treatise on power. These are drafted in to demonstrate that the task of a strategic manager is to *win*. Strategy, they imply, is cleverly marshalling resources in order to outwit your opponent. For sure, running a business, whether for profit or surplus, can be turbulent, but is it really like this? Managers *today* are facing the issues of the 21st century. The analogy of historical conflict and war might be useful, but not directly and not in the way described above.

For example, we can learn something about the roots of business strategy from the Cold War period *after* the Second World

War. This period contained valuable lessons about how to win at peace and prosperity rather than at war. These lessons have less to do with tactics used in battles fought or the anecdotes of old soldiers than with a clear understanding of how to organise and operate in a context of change and development.

By 1945 the world was ready for a really radical transformation. Old ways of doing things had come to an end and rigid social structures had been turned upside down. Nearly all the world's major economies needed rebuilding. Politically, economically and socially, the world needed to roll up its sleeves, work out what to do and get on with it. Global conflict had necessitated the development of great planning skills, so there was no shortage of experts to create and implement new policy. The ideological and military arms race of the 1950s certainly had its dark side, but this was also counter-balanced by the desire to bring nations together. This triggered agreements for trade and new technologies for production and innovation. By the late 1950s these macroeconomic forces had discovered a brand new microeconomic concept – the consumer. A hungry consumer, too.

We have been relying on finding new consumers ever since. The result? New markets – and mass markets. In a world where economic growth was seen as the best way of avoiding another global military conflict, every incentive for business to meet needs was encouraged. The most effective strategy for this was the gradual removal of barriers to trade, which created a much more open type of competition.

when you start facing real competition, you need to plan

When you start facing real competition, or when you see brand new markets opening up, you need to plan.

 **tip**

Strategy should be the means to achieving a goal, never the goal itself.

Since the 1960s we have seen an incredible boom in the number of companies.[1] As these organisations grow, they become more complex. As economies grow, they also become more complex. It is no coincidence that many of the founding voices in the development of strategy and planning for corporations and business emerged in the post-war period of planning economic growth. The 1950s was the decade of public planning in Europe and North America and, eventually, corporate planning became a management science, which found a new home in the university business schools.

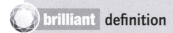 **definition**

Strategy

This is the process by which an entity or organisation sets a direction and implements a plan to reach its goals, chief of which is usually its own continued survival.

Beyond this definition, it gets tricky. Why? Well, what an organisation plans to do may not be the same as what it ends up actually doing. Try this experiment: if you can, ask your CEO or boss to recall what was the organisation's strategy or plan five years ago. Then ask them what they actually did. Were they the same?

it seems that luck can also be a strategy

Equally, what now looks like the result of a carefully thought-through strategic plan may originally have come about as the result of a random event or chance (someone saw an opportunity and grabbed it and it paid off). It seems that luck can also be a strategy.

There have been many definitions of strategy and the classical view is 'the big plan'. Alfred Chandler, an influential Harvard business history professor, was in this mode when he wrote in 1962:

Strategy is the determination of the basic long-term goals of an enterprise, and the adoption of courses of action and the allocation of resources necessary for carrying out these goals.[2]

This view is quite mechanistic; it says you need the structures in place before anything else, and then you measure progress against (usually) your budget. In other words, only with the right management and organisation can a firm move forward.

Our view of strategy has moved on from this. During the 1970s and 1980s, economic theory began to be used as a basis for understanding how markets and industries behave (note the language here – organisations behave and misbehave – just like people do) in relation to its external environment. Strategy began to look more like the science of positioning yourself correctly against your competitors, within the constraints of whatever industry you were in. It is not a huge leap from this to scrutinising those things you have got that your competitors do not, analysing which ones add value, and then focusing your strategy on managing those resources well. Again, organisations were supposed to be a bit like people in this regard – work out what your strengths and weaknesses are against others and compete.

Lately, strategy has also started to be a question of adaptation and learning. Now the organisation looks a bit like a student, learning as it grows (up).

brilliant tip

All strategy definitions contribute to a full picture. As you become more aware, you will begin to appreciate that everything you do as a manager has (or could have) a strategic link.

In a business school, strategy is seen as the subject that brings the functional courses such as finance, marketing and operations together. Functional subjects generally move into the curriculum from business but with strategy it sort of went the opposite way. Relatively few organisations have staff whose *only* job is strategy, or departments whose *only* function is planning, yet there is not one business school without faculty dedicated to the subject.

Not everyone will feel strategy is remote and academic. If you are a start-up entrepreneur, your company is brand new and, frankly, *everything* you do is strategy. Similarly, if you are an Apple, Shell or Wal-Mart, you are sitting on global businesses with turnovers larger than the GDPs of some countries and you are most certainly going to employ *a lot* of specialists and experts (including external consultants with MBAs) for strategic planning and implementation. But for the vast majority, life is about responding to the challenge of getting from today to tomorrow; strategy is either someone else's concern or a barrier to you doing your job.

Why it matters

Henry Mintzberg (more from him later) makes an interesting distinction between *deliberate* strategies (i.e. plans, or what an organisation *intends* to happen) and *unintended* strategies (i.e. pattern, or reaction to whatever is going on at the time).[3] If we are honest, says Mintzberg, we should admit that we muddle along somewhere between the two because organisations never have complete control. But nor do they drift entirely without aim. Management is about being a more effective and far-sighted muddler. Slightly in contrast to this, Michael E. Porter (about whom you will also hear) believes more in the rational and analytical influence of market economics. For him and for many others who have echoed his work, strategy is almost exclusively a question of *positioning* your offering in such a way that you maintain a competitive advantage over your rivals.

You may have the impression that there are as many definitions of strategy as there are strategists! Do not panic, some common points do emerge. People generally agree that strategy is:

- **necessary and important:** there are many different flavours of how you might do it but if you do not know what you are doing, someone else will take your customer;
- **future- and goal-oriented:** it is a link from the present to the future;
- **a connection from the present to the past:** this can be a double-edged sword because past experience both informs and restricts how an organisation sees the present;
- **dynamic:** it is a dance performed by all parts and by all people in an organisation. Successful implementation is cultural as much as it is analytical, and iterative as much as it is set in stone.

Regardless of your philosophy, no strategy statement will be clear unless it can ask and answer these questions:

- What business are we in?
- What should we do to create value in our business in the future?

Steering an organisation in the right direction is not easy. Sometimes that is because we have made it even more confusing ourselves. There is no shortage of consultants to offer advice and some – the Boston Consulting Group, Bain and McKinsey being three examples – have contributed a lot to our vocabulary. Your skill as a brilliant business strategist will come partly from understanding these perspectives, as well as from finding your own way.

brilliant tip

Make a list of strategic issues that your organisation is facing at the moment. Rank them from most important to least important. What do you think makes these issues strategic?

Large, commercial corporations are a phenomenon of the 20th century. Many are products of waves of consolidation and nearly all originally grew from expanding their production resources to feed sales. That was more or less the only strategy you needed, and you did not need much sophisticated corporate planning and policy. Henry Ford's famous 1918 statement 'any colour as long as it's black' made some sense because demand from the American public was so far behind supply that his focus on assembly was the only thing that mattered (in those days marketing was less important than establishing production). This shot Ford ahead of the dozens of small, bespoke car manufacturers springing up around them (names now long forgotten).[4] It is unlikely that his was a strategy in our modern sense.[5]

At first, planning was an activity conducted mainly by government or by those corporations that needed to make investment decisions that would bear fruit many years into the future. Such large businesses became a legitimate vehicle for wealth creation for investors via public share ownership, and strategy spread to more specialist departments located far away from the everyday activities of the middle manager.

Early strategic thinking owed much to engineering and pro-cess-driven views of management and business, and was fuelled by capital markets supplying consumer-driven booms in world markets. As those markets became more sophisti-cated, and as more regional economies opened up to private enterprise, competition became more intense and consumers could exercise more power of choice. In other words, they could choose *not* to beat a path to your door. You now needed a commercial plan if you wanted to continue to please your stockholders.[6]

Strategic drift: change in a changing world

We love to say that our world is constantly changing, and it is. And so do our ideas and practices of business and manage-ment. Change is like the sea – when a big wave hits, change is dramatic; a new invention or a terrible calamity can impact everyone.

The storms are generally what grab the headlines. We tend to forget that, most of the time, there are no storms. Change usu-ally happens at a much slower rate, like the steady but irresistible coming in and going out of the tide.

change is like the sea

An agile company can act to stay ahead of the predictable rises and falls, even to the point of reinventing itself when it wants. However, change often usually creeps up on us and, especially if there is a business model that has proved reasonably successful, companies may lose sight of the movement around them to find they are caught high and dry when the tide goes out (or drowned when it comes in). This gap is called **strategic drift.**

There may have been no obvious disaster or crisis but some-times a business can find that its current model is no longer sustainable. On rare occasions, a firm may no longer be viable and can even end up lacking the means to continue trading.

 **definition**

Strategic drift

This is when an organisation gradually loses its way over time. It can be hard to spot because profits may be good and feedback from existing customers may be positive, but these can mask the fact that, at a fundamental level, the industry or sector has moved on and you have not noticed.

By focusing on email functionality, Canadian tech. company Research in Motion (RIM, now called BlackBerry) surfed a wave of popularity in mobile office technology, and reigned supreme until the rise of the smartphone and the downloadable app. By the time they realised something was up, in 2012, it was too late – the drift had begun several years earlier. The board of the company was split between those who wanted to join the touchscreen crowd and those who wanted to remain with a keyboard.[7]

What will be the next BlackBerry? Will the internal combustion engine be electrocuted? Or the USB stick become obscured by the Cloud? A sense of being out of touch should be a more common starting point for strategic change than the shock to the system of a financial crisis, or any other rapid driver. The most difficult step may be admitting that drift has happened in the first place. When an organisation tells itself it has a good business model, and is profitable, few people are willing to rock the boat by saying anything is wrong. This is because you would also be questioning one or more core assumptions.

risk-aversion may itself be risky

Many companies continue in the hope that their strategy will pay off and, generally, managers are risk-averse. In a world where technology is shortening every business cycle, risk-aversion may itself be risky.

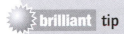 **tip**

Your greatest barrier to change may be that one or more of the core assumptions of your business has become out of touch with current reality.

When (*if*) drift is noticed, what might happen next is:

1 Panic. The organisation starts searching for a solution. Heads may roll as those with governance responsibility attempt to create a new agenda and direction.

2 An internal crisis of this sort may have several rounds of strategic soul searching, a series of awaydays, ceaseless numbers of top-down initiatives and endless rounds of reorganisation. This can be a very unsettling experience for everyone concerned.

Of course, there may be many factors involved in drift over time. For instance, take a look at what happened to HMV.

 **example**

HMV

Slow but steady changes in a business environment can often be overlooked when organisations are doing well. HMV opened its first record store in London's Oxford Street in 1921 and became an established and successful retailer of music and musical equipment through the 1930s and 40s. With the advent of popular music and a youth market in the 1960s, it began a rapid expansion that continued for two decades. Its Oxford Street flagship store was, for a while, the world's largest when it opened in 1986, and HMV ▶

continued to build on this model, peaking at 320 outlets by the end of the 1990s. By then, the portfolio included the Waterstones and Dillons bookshop chains. Whilst HMV had once been the biggest player in a booming market, by 2012 it was making a loss on an annual turnover that had fallen to slightly under £1 billion. By the start of 2013, HMV Group Plc entered administration, effectively ceasing to trade by 2014.

What had the management of the company missed? Arguably, indicators of strategic drift should have been addressed when the company was doing well, but it focused its efforts on expansion in high street retail and, later, in music venues. It did not see the repercussions of the move to digital technology. When vinyl went into decline, HMV's core business assumption – that it sells pre-recorded music, face-to-face – was reinforced by the huge profit margins it made on physical sales of CDs, at that time the new technology. Senior management had some of their prejudices about the impact of the internet reinforced when the dotcom stock bubble burst in the early 2000s, so there was no willingness to believe that their powerful retail business could be threatened, as long as they continued making intelligent, incremental changes. By the time falling sales figures began to look irreversible, it was too late – the strategy was not sustainable.

Under new management from HILCO, HMV is now slowly in recovery. In early 2015 it overtook Amazon as the UK's largest retailer of CDs and records. Its slogan 'The home of entertainment since 1921' hints at a return to the original brand proposition, though the move online still remains a challenge.[8]

For many years HMV was a very successful company, good at responding to occasional innovations in the business environment. At the same time, not only did it fail to notice that small changes (mostly too small to make a big fuss over) were beginning to add up, it also failed to see that the rate and pace of change was accelerating (mostly from digital technology).

strategy reaches out and touches everything

When push came to shove, they were not ready for the online world. Strategy reaches out and touches everything – past, present and future. The lesson here is that, when things do start to go wrong, you need to get back to the basics of what makes a business flow.

Even if you spot strategic drift, many questions arise. Should your new strategy be set out in a plan or should it emerge as you go? Does your competition threaten you or define you? Should your organisation's structure change to fit your strategy or should your strategy be based around your structure? Should you work only to maximise profit or act in the interests of a wider set of stakeholders?

Finding answers to all these questions is not easy. A good first step is working out what sort of issue you are up against. There are a number of types:

Puzzles: situations that have a solution that has not yet been worked out.

Dilemmas: puzzles with two possible solutions, each with its own disadvantages. Neither wins hands down.

Compromises: agreement on the least-worst outcome where all sides agree to give up something they value.

Paradoxes: two or more seemingly contradictory situations appear true at the same time and, through time, even though, logically, that looks impossible.

Navigating these is all about management decision making and thinking. With such a wide scope it is no wonder that, if you are a manager, strategy is one of the most interesting and dynamic subjects you can master.

So let us take a look at you.

How to be a brilliant strategist

Have you noticed that people love offering you advice on what to do and how to behave? I doubt this is much use when it comes to developing your skills as a strategist. After all, sometimes success in strategy comes when you do exactly the opposite of what everyone says you should be doing. So, I cannot tell you what to do, but I can share three insights on how to think like a strategist:

1 **The first step is awareness.** You cannot change something that you have not noticed. First, you must have the skills to identify that there is a strategic issue.

brilliant tip

First, know yourself. Then, and only then, will you really be able to make a difference in planning, implementing and evaluating corporate strategy or business unit strategy.

2 **Be prepared to abandon your old maps.** I love looking at old maps. They give you a sense of what the world must have looked like in the past. But strategists need to explore the territory with fresh eyes as if seeing it for the first time. Analytical skills can be useful, but they will not lead to generating novelty or to solutions to any problem that requires you to reinterpret what you already know. For this you need imagination and thinking skills.

3 **You can and should be a role model.** Just being smart or being a risk-taker is not enough. Nor is being good at ordering people around. You also need the right intention (which is the right energy and the right mission and purpose).

'Your first and foremost job as a leader is to take charge of your own energy and then help to orchestrate the energy of those around you.'

Peter Drucker, management consultant

This is a great quote from the person who more or less invented the field of management. Awareness, courage to see and positive energy – these are valuable lessons to learn. Day-to-day management is about maintaining structure and stability and the easiest route to a solution. It looks for answers. Strategic management, on the other hand, wants to interrupt things. It generates new ideas and possibilities and new spaces to move into. It looks for questions.

 **tip**

To look for the right questions you need to read the signals that generate them. This requires **business intelligence** (the tools used for turning raw data into useful knowledge) and **business acumen** (the thinking skills needed to apply knowledge for a positive outcome).

Here are three more tips about how to be a brilliant business strategist that I want you to keep in mind as you read on:

1 **We are always a part of what we encounter.** Your ability to learn from the world as you go along is a crucial part of becoming a strategist. In management, think of every business problem as an opportunity to work on your own personal issues at the same time.

2 **Do not be afraid to get things wrong.** The brilliant business strategist sees ideas that others have missed, but

there is no guarantee that when you try something new your ideas will be successful. If you accept that failure is part of moving forward, then you will have learnt one of the most valuable lessons.

3 **As a strategist, you need to practise and master two powerful states.** The first is as a *listener*. When you listen in order to understand, you get to embrace whatever is going on, without baggage or self-delusions. The second is the energy you use when you are *giving direction* (this is not the same as telling others what to do in a top-down way). When you are calm and clear-minded, you will be able to communicate this energy naturally and your decisiveness and your plans will be evident to those around you.

When you look at strategic issues, remember that the stuff you see going wrong in business is usually a *symptom* or *outcome* of the actual problem, not the problem itself.

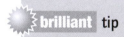 **tip**

Great management is often a question of the right energy, not just the right actions.

brilliant recap

Here is a summary of the main ideas that you can apply or bring to your own practice as a manager:

● Always keep asking yourself what strategy is. Your ideas and definitions will constantly evolve, and you must be open to as many views as you can. You will find your own understanding.

● Although, occasionally, it can be rapid and catastrophic, change is often a slow and steady process. Many organisations drift into strategic dilemmas.

● Keep an eye on whether your business is still in touch with its market. Have you kept up with how things have changed?

● A strategist is always asking themselves who they are. The art of strategy involves a very clear sense of self-knowledge.

In the next chapter we will look at how you go about understanding your business and analysing your external business environment.

References

[1] No one knows for sure how many companies there are in the world, but in 2013 Dun & Bradstreet listed 230 million on its database.

[2] Chandler, A.D., Jr. (1962) *Strategy and Structure*. Cambridge, MA: MIT Press, p. 13.

[3] Mintzberg, H. (1994) *The Rise and Fall of Strategic Planning*. Harlow: Prentice Hall.

[4] The family tree of the US automobile industry now has only three branches (Ford, Chrysler and GM) but about 7,000 roots formed by independent pioneers and entrepreneurs.

[5] An amusing footnote to the Ford success story is the opinion of the President of the Michigan Savings Bank when Ford approached for a loan, 'The horse is here today, but the automobile is only a novelty – a fad.'

[6] Henry Ford himself never really came round to this way of thinking, but others did.

[7] Silcoff, C., McNish, J. and Ladurantaye, S. (2013) 'Inside the fall of BlackBerry: How the smartphone inventor failed to adapt', *The Globe and Mail*. [Online] 27 September. Available from: http://www.theglobeandmail.com/report-on-business/the-inside-story-of-why-blackberry-is-failing/article14563602/?page=all

[8] Compiled by the author. Sources include:
Beeching, P. (2013) 'Why did HMV fail?', *Guardian*. [Online] 15 January. Available from: http://www.theguardian.com/commentisfree/2013/jan/15/why-did-hmv-fail
Ruddick, G. (2015) 'HMV reclaims its position as Britain's biggest music retailer', *The Telegraph*. [Online] 16 January. Available from:

http://www.telegraph.co.uk/finance/newsbysector/retailand
consumer/11348287/HMV-reclaims-its-position-as-Britains-biggest-
music-retailer.html

Vizard, S. (2014) 'Can HMV turn improving brand sentiment into
sales?', *Marketing Week* [Online] 4 April.

CHAPTER 2

Strategic issues

No man is an island entire of itself; every man is a piece of the continent, a part of the main.

John Donne, *Meditations XVII, Devotions upon Emergent Occasions*

How this chapter will help you

Clarity of mission and vision for the organisation is an important function of management and leadership. This chapter will help you understand how to analyse an industry or sector, locate your position in reference to others, and identify the drivers for change in your environment.

Introduction

What is a strategic issue? More precisely, what is a strategic issue for *you* because what counts as a challenge will vary from one organisation to the next and from one person to the next.[1] Strategic issues will be different for:

- a multinational enterprise (MNE) with many business units and portfolios of products and services, versus a small to medium-size enterprise (SME) with perhaps only one or two;

- a manufacturing business versus a service organisation, where the basis and components of competitive advantage may be very different;

- the private versus the public or non-profit sector – even when not-for-profits have paying customers, the organisational mission and purpose may be very different; it may even be pre-determined by others;

- a risk-averse manager versus a risk-taker, a democratic leader versus an autocrat . . . and so on.

no organisation exists in a vacuum

Issues may come in all shapes and sizes but the methods used by strategists to identify them generally do not.

No organisation exists in a vacuum, there is *always* a context. The most straightforward one, of course, is between you and your customers. There are many more, though, such as with shareholders, regulators, suppliers, employees and competitors. Without these as context life would be not only dull, it would also be meaningless. What is more, your organisation is as vital to their meaning as they are to yours. This mutually arising web of connections is dynamic over time and few organisations (including the very big ones) can say with precision how their immediate environment will change, even in the short term.

So we know that strategic issues are not simple. We know, too, that they are not easy. If they were, companies would not struggle to react to change and they would achieve all their goals. And struggle they do. A strategic issue is one that must be addressed because to ignore it would put the future of the organisation at risk. This chapter is about identifying such issues primarily at the corporate level where a business interacts with the world beyond its boundaries (issues at the level above this are part of **network strategy**). It starts by asking what business you are in and why. Then it moves on to what you want your business to look like in the future.

'Crisis? What crisis?' Greiner's Growth Cycle

Before we set about choosing a strategic direction, there is an important point to make and it has something to do with the fact that organisations mimic organisms. Businesses all around the world vary a lot in what they do but are, mostly, set up in the same way. They all start as a gleam in someone's eye and come into the world in a sort of legal maternity ward as a start-up. Carefully nurtured, they grow and learn to find their way around. They age, mature and (unless some serious plastic surgery is undertaken) eventually they start to look and act their age. In the end, they must either change or give way to the next generation. In other words, an organisation will tend to experience distinct phases as it grows and matures and will face some difficult choices as it does. These stages can determine what sort of issues become strategic.

American academic Larry Greiner proposed in 1972 that successful enterprises go through five distinct phases of growth.[2] Success in each phase sooner or later results in a particular type of crisis. To move into the next phase, the organisation must change what it does and how it does it, sometimes even requiring a change at the top, because the most powerful objection to doing things differently often emanates from there. Table 2.1 lists each of these stages and crises.

Table 2.1 Greiner's phases of enterprise crisis and growth

Phases (ca. 3 to 15 years)	Evolution . . .	Leads to . . . revolution
1 (the organisation is small and young)	Creativity The company is informal, driven by the vision of its founders, who also take on the majority of the management. The drive is to sell.	Crisis of leadership With too much to do, the founders ask if the organisation now needs professionals to share the workload.

▶

Phases (ca. 3 to 15 years)	Evolution . . .	Leads to . . . revolution
2	Direction The company becomes more efficient and more centralised. Control becomes more formal and is from the centre. Strategic issues include whether to stay in one area or expand and diversify.	Crisis of autonomy Diversity brings a struggle between following central procedures and the pursuit of local initiatives. Neither senior managers nor middle managers are used to the idea of moving decisions downward.
3	Decentralisation Markets expand through strong local management, scope increases, divisions and sub-sections appear, (often by acquisition) and senior management become remote.	Crisis of control The centre reacts by enforcing centralisation and budget control of diverse local units, centralised planning returns, efficiencies amongst diversified units is sought, everyone has to justify their activity.
4	Coordination Standardisation of all operations, creation of set methods. Management focus shifts to the firm's good name and reputation.	Crisis of red tape Has the organisation become bogged down in its own rules and procedures? How can it rekindle the spirit of innovation?
5 (the organisation is large and mature)	Collaboration To counter the red-tape culture, senior management now work in matrix teams, strategic decisions are facilitated using specialist consultants, the organisation hunts for innovative leaders from lower down.	(Crisis of . . . ?) Focus moves beyond the organisation to alliances across an industry.

Successful transition from one stage to the next is not a given. An organisation can become static and still survive, or it can become the target of a takeover, merger or acquisition and disappear. Or it can simply fail.

Organisational purpose: VMOST

VMOST stands for vision – mission – objectives – strategy – tactics. Popular as a management shortcut in the 1980s and 1990s, it has rather fallen out of fashion in the wake of high-profile corporate failures of organisations with strong statements of values, all led by visionaries with missions that operated double standards in their practice. Remember how Enron was once *the* company of innovation and growth? Everyone admired it and wanted to work there. It, too, defined itself – outwardly – by its vision and values, which in 2000 included the memorable section:

We believe in respect for the rights of all individuals and are committed to promoting an environment characterised by dignity and mutual respect for employees, customers, contractors, suppliers, partners, community members, and representatives of all levels of government.[3]

As we now know, despite the PR, inwardly Enron was being run corruptly and fraudulently to bankruptcy by its management, who were no respecters of the dignity of stakeholders. When the only outcome that counts is the return on the bottom line, corporate vision and mission statements may end up with a poor reputation. Mission statements with hidden agendas deserve a bad rap. On the other hand, statements that match (more or less – remember, they are aspirational) actual practice can serve a real purpose. Brevity may help. Virgin Atlantic Airways, founded in 1984, has a very short mission statement that reflects succinctly both the competitive nature of the long-haul passenger business sector where it competes, and the liberating human goals it aspires to as part of the Virgin Group of companies.

Stop for a moment – how does that strike you? Do not forget what I said earlier about acknowledging that we see the world through the lens of our prejudices and beliefs. Virgin Atlantic Airways operates alongside Virgin Holidays, and they form Virgin Atlantic, which is jointly owned by Richard Branson's Virgin Group (51 per cent) and Delta Airways (49 per cent). Virgin Atlantic Airways maintains a fleet of 39 aircraft and made profits of £14.1 million on a turnover of nearly £3 billion in 2014. In 2013 it launched what turned out to be a short-lived UK domestic service called Little Red. In 2015 Virgin announced it was winding this business up. As with its long-haul arm, Little Red was aimed firmly at the premium or business traveller. The failure of that venture will not be seen at Virgin as failure, but as learning.

In fact, Virgin has pioneered many innovations over the years to stay ahead of rivals on some of the world's most fiercely competitive routes. In an industry of tight margins, Virgin's entrepreneurial heritage and energy comes across strongly.

Great vision and mission need not necessarily be written down to exist. Compare Virgin's 21st century approach with the Marinelli Bell Foundry, a small business established in Italy in the 14th century and still a family-run enterprise, employing 12 people.[4] On their website there is no neatly worded mission statement or detailed analysis of a carefully presented strategy. But you will not need these to appreciate the purpose of the business, which rings out clearly through nearly a millennium's worth of crafting bells history (mostly for the Vatican). Virgin and Marinelli appear to have clarity of purpose and can say with some confidence what business they are in. Yet notice how neither is stuck to the idea of purpose being the destination; there is no 'we do this only until . . . ' – the doing is the goal.

brilliant questions

Find out if there is a statement of purpose in the organisation you work for. How was this created, how is it refreshed and how is it communicated? If there is no such statement, how does anyone know the purpose?

Author and TED speaker Simon Sinek has helped fuel a resurgence of interest in organisational purpose.[5] He presents the *why* of your business as the basis for the *how* and the *what*. I would add that knowing *why* your organisation exists is important for two reasons:

1 Unless *you* founded the organisation where you work, *someone else* held the reason for starting it. The company grew from those ideas before you joined it, possibly many management generations ago. You will, in time, become part of that story, but the original purpose must be acknowledged, especially if your future thinking involves a major change in direction. You are, in a sense, a steward of the original purpose.

2 More pragmatically, in order to undertake assessment of strategic issues (or select strategic objectives) you must *be clear about what counts as a strategic issue* in your industry or in your market. And, if you cannot do that, you will not know what action to take. Without planned action, you cannot measure the success or otherwise of your performance. Without performance, you will not know whether you are attaining the company's purpose. It is a cycle.

Once you know what the original idea behind your business or organisation was, you can begin to observe how its culture has refined over time, what has been added (mergers, acquisitions?), what core skills have been developed and what it is currently capable of. To begin this, most people adopt two types of strategic analysis. In Part 2, we will look at analysing the *internal* environment of the organisation, but right now let us start with the *external* world of the industry, sector or market.

 **tip**

Your business is defined by your choice of customer.

Industry analysis

As we have seen, purpose and strategy are very closely linked. A strategic issue is a challenge to purpose. But where do such strategic issues come from? Here are three answers:

1　They emerge from what is going on outside your organisation in the wider business environment (not just in your industry). Changes in this external world could make your purpose redundant *or* could mean that *now* is the time to act to achieve your dreams.

2　They are shaped by you. They are the result of your analysis of your competitive position and your relationship with any rivals in the same competing space as you.

3　They come from how you organise and nurture those resources that your competitors do not.

Issues come at you from two directions. There are those inherent in the structure of the **industry** (often called the supply side), and those in the nature of the **marketplace** (or demand side). Strategists use both perspectives: an *external* analysis of the drivers affecting an industry and an *internal* analysis of the competitive position within that industry.

Let us look at the external world first. Is yours an industry worth being in? Or, put another way, is your industry *attractive*?

 **brilliant** definition

Industry

This is a complex group of companies that make or provide a similar set of products or services (in any type of business) to meet a given market need.

Attractive here means that the structure of your industry makes it possible for a return on investment higher than the cost of the capital being invested. Some industries, just by their very nature, will give better margins than others. That sounds good, and it is, but it makes them more attractive to competitors as well. For example, few analysts would advise you to start an airline because, even if you had the money to invest, the operating margins in that industry are very low. And, if you could not earn more with your money than you would somewhere else, then it might not be such a good industry.

Do a little bit of research of your own area. What kind of industry or sector do you work in? Are players generally making good margins or are they paper thin? Do you think this has any consequence for whether new competitors would enter your market?

Consumers do not usually have needs that can be met by just one industry. All industries are inter-connected and inter-dependent.

all industries are inter-connected and inter-dependent

In order to buy a new pair of shoes, you certainly need a shoe industry to sell you the footwear, but your shoe-seller is reliant on there being a shipping, wholesaling, distribution and logistics sector to move their goods, an agricultural and livestock sector for direct raw materials (leather does not grow on trees), an energy sector for any indirect raw materials (plastics) or power supply, an education sector to train people with the right skills, a banking sector to provide liquidity and finance, an advertising industry, too, and, of course, a retail sector (itself dependent on many other industries) to sell in, and so on. All these industries are, in turn, consumers and suppliers of the necessary goods and services from other industries. And every industry operates in a wider economic context, which we can see through a PESTEL.

PESTEL

When performing an industry level analysis, the best place to start is with one of the most robust frameworks in strategic thinking – PESTEL, which stands for:

Political: what governments are doing in terms of setting levels of taxation, passing laws or setting regulations that corporations must follow, whether or not they are stable, how they interact with other governments in international relations and trade, how they manage fiscal policy and interest rates, and their policies on social welfare.

Economic: macro measurements that track business cycles, central bank policies on interest rates and inflation (the link to the political is here), levels of unemployment and levels of disposable income.

Social: the way that wealth is distributed, the demographics of the population in a given area, education levels, attitudes to a whole range of issues (including the environment), and cultural signifiers, such as social mobility.

Technological: the reliance on information technology most businesses have sometimes masks the possibilities at the edge of new developments and discoveries. We may also focus on the ways in which government enables spending on infrastructure, and the amounts devoted by organisations to research and development, not forgetting the social side of how we treat the by-products and waste from these processes.

Environmental: how economic activity is regulated regarding its impact on the environment, the commercial effects and costs of waste management, exploitation of various sources of energy, social attitudes to the balance between economic growth and the sustainability of the biosphere.

Legal: laws in place to enable and control completion, regulations as they affect employment and health and safety within the organisation (as well as up and down the supply chain), and the legal obligations or liabilities around the safety of products and services.

PESTEL is broad, but not necessarily global. Despite the globalisation of many industries, the world is still a remarkably localised place. At the same time, every local context is part of a wider one, and you can apply this to your business model, even if you are self-employed or a small business. Whatever your size, you are affected by macro forces. All parts of a PESTEL are interlinked but organisations will usually identify priorities in some areas over others. The test for your analysis is to ask *'So what?'* in each section. If there is a high impact, then you need to act.

> if there is a high impact, then you need to act

brilliant tip

Concentrate your attention only on those elements of a PESTEL that have both a high probability of happening *and* a high impact on your business.

PESTEL analyses will vary. One for the highly regulated pharmaceutical industry may look completely different from one prepared for oil and gas, which, in turn, may look nothing like the environment of the music industry. Whatever the differences, PESTEL has factors that end up influencing what happens internally in an organisation. The secret to using PESTEL for identifying your strategic issues lies – in part – in asking good questions in each of the categories. But what makes for a good question depends on what you know about your organisation and what you know about your competition.

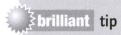

tip

Do not define your company by what is on the inside. You are just as defined by the industry you are part of and the market segment(s) you are targeting.

Let us deal with the competitor question next.

Porter's Five Forces

Conventional wisdom is that competition is about winning – beating your opponents and maintaining a dominant position over them for a prolonged length of time. Is this correct? Yes and no. Yes, this is how a lot of managers see it and they act accordingly, and there are some very influential opinion leaders who agree. But also no, the relationship you have with your competitors (and who you define as your competitors) is not necessarily so black and white. For example, competing organisations may cooperate, form alliances, or at least tolerate each other in order to preserve the attractiveness of their industry. And you can learn from your competitors as well.

you can learn from your competitors as well

The most important concept within competitive strategy is the notion of **differentiation.** This is why you will not find a book on strategy that does not mention Michael Porter's influence on how the success or failure of a firm is a matter of finding a competing position in an industry with regard to a number of forces that define it. Not everyone agrees with him fully, but it is really worth knowing what Porter's ideas are (if only to have a starting point).

 **tip**

For success, an industry must be attractive enough to be profitable and a firm must be good enough to keep doing well, despite others competing against it.

There are five forces at work in determining industry attractiveness. If all of them are favourable, the rewards for all players are likely to be big. Where they work against you, your margins and your profits may always be low – almost regardless of what you do. To understand why, take a look at the forces (which will be *high, medium* or *low*):

Rivalry between firms: are you constantly keeping an eye on certain companies in your space? If the main players in the market are well balanced in terms of their size and organisation, or if consumers can easily switch, then rivalry will be high. In some locations, energy companies, supermarkets, mobile phone operators and automobile manufacturers face intense competition and this shapes their strategy.

Threat of new entrants: if it is relatively easy for anyone else to enter your chosen market, then the threat you face is high, forcing you to compete. In an industry with high barriers, new entrants are less likely and less important in your strategy. There are lots of things that might hold back new entrants, ranging from economies of scale that existing players may have achieved (usually via lower costs), to government policies that actively block or encourage competition.

Bargaining power of buyers: can your customers influence you easily? If you have only a few big customers, or if they are very sensitive to changes in price, then this aspect will almost certainly have a high importance to your strategy. If there are more customers (buyers) than suppliers, then they have more influence. If it would cost them a lot to switch, then, arguably, you have more influence over them (think here of the way that Apple has built its business).

Bargaining powers of suppliers: if you depend on particular suppliers that you cannot easily or cheaply switch away from, or if your supplier could easily do what your company does, then this force would be high. It is also high if your supplier could dump you and go to another customer.

Threat of substitutes: a customer's needs are not always matched to a particular brand. If I want a fizzy drink, only companies making fizzy drinks are going to be able to help. If I am thirsty, then, potentially, other drinks companies may compete (note how Coca-Cola and Pepsi acquired mineral water brands). This much is obvious. But when a need can also be met by completely different products or services, the attractiveness of the whole industry may be in question. If my need is entertainment, then potentially many different products or services could satisfy it. And if I have limited funds, I may be making hard choices about what I spend it on. Tastes as well as needs change over time and this force may be one reason there is so much management literature on innovation.

 example

The global hotel industry

The hotel and motel industry was worth about £350 billion in 2013, with annual growth in excess of 7 per cent forecast over the next five years, despite the global economic downturn and regional conflicts.[6] The international market is dominated by a relatively small number of large and very competitive players, whilst local and regional markets are catered for by a wide range of niche and small independents. 75 per cent of industry revenue is generated by guests travelling for leisure, whilst the rest comes from the business segment.

Major chains include Accor (France), InterContinental Hotels Group (IHG) (UK), Best Western (USA) and Wyndham Worldwide (USA). Each company operates under a slightly different business model and reaches different segments with branded chains. IHG, for instance, had revenues of £1.2 billion in 2013 and its brands include InterContinental Hotels and Resorts, Crowne Plaza, Holiday Inn and Holiday Inn Express. Unlike its main competitors, the vast majority of its 4,600 hotels are franchises.

In terms of Porter's Five Forces, this is a mature and competitive industry. *Rivalry* amongst existing players is high, so value-added offers and loyalty schemes, alongside diversification to broaden the offering, are common-place. *Buyers* have moderate influence, being numerous and sensitive to offers on price. Because they usually have plenty of options, there are few barriers to switching. On the other hand, the bigger chains can easily pick up other customers. *Suppliers* have little power relative to the big chains, since they are mostly local and cannot operate with the same economies of scale. At the same time, the chains depend on high quality of staff, good sources of fixtures and fittings and, most importantly, IT systems. In these areas, the suppliers can have much more influence. The weakened travel sector since 2008 has probably held back the threat of *new entrants* in direct competition, whilst geographic spread evens out any regional falls in demand (plus there has been some consolidation). Buyers demand a consistent experience in branded hotel chains. Small-scale hotels operate in their own marketplace, though they are as sensitive to different market segments as their larger counterparts.

Aggregator hotel websites, such as Booking.com, have become influential in the industry as search engines used by buyers, largely replacing the high-street travel agents (who have moved out, gone online or moved to niche segments). Consumer behaviour by travellers reviewing hotels online through sites such as TripAdvisor (buyer bargaining power), means hotel chains cannot ignore examples of poor service. One aspect of the industry that is less predictable is the rapid growth in popularity, thanks again to the Web, of *substitute* forms of accommodation, the largest being Airbnb, which offers private rentals in people's homes or in privately owned apartments.

The Five Forces framework has been around for a long time, and that means people often like taking potshots at it. Some say it has not kept up with shifts in the global economy (emerging markets) or the immense impact of the internet. Others point out that it is only a static snapshot of a moment in time and this limits you seeing things in the long view (this is true for a lot of strategy tools). Porter himself points out that many variables are not included in this picture, and that each industry has different drivers that develop over time.

What do you think?

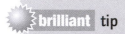 **tip**

Think about your organisation and its market position through this lens and see if you can identify anything that crosses over with a PESTEL analysis of your wider business environment.

The industry life cycle

Probably every business tries to convince itself that it will be around forever. Of course, this is not the case. Nine out of the top ten largest companies in the 1995 Fortune 500 list now no longer exist, have been merged into other businesses or are reduced considerably in size. Whole industries (I am using the word very broadly here, not just manufacturing) as well as organisations and products change over time, as was noticed by Michael Porter, who mapped industry cycles into four phases in his 1985 book, *Competitive Strategy*.[7]

> **Introduction:** things are messy and unclear. Perhaps few outsiders even see that there is an industry yet. There is comparatively little competition, but plenty of innovation (risk-taking), some of which may soon pay off. And plenty of

failures, too. No economies of scale, meaning high costs. *Key success factors: innovation in design, building awareness, financing.*

Growth: plenty of interest and new entrants getting in on the act, agreements on standardisation around dominant technology (if needed), a constant shortage of capacity as supply struggles to meet new demand, expansion by export to less-developed markets. *Key success factors: access to distribution, better design, branding, rapid innovation.*

Maturity: demand is at its highest, increasing awareness by consumers for quality or price, incremental improvements in technology, capacity demands are met, production may move to low-cost locations, fewer players as consolidation sets in, price wars as innovation declines. *Key success factors: return on capital employed (ROCE), efficiency of production and control of costs.*

Decline: demand has moved on from what this industry produces, very little value in differentiation as a strategy, over-capacity (which may be global) as price is now the only driver, many exits but possibility of niche positions for remaining players. *Key success factors: control of costs, diversification or divestment, small-scale and focused innovation to niche markets for survivors.*

Industry life cycles are about more internal factors. Many worthy organisations have found that the ground beneath them changes as demand falls away or moves to other parts of the world.

brilliant questions

Where are you balanced against your competitors in industry terms? Where is your industry in its life cycle? What would it cost you to exit this industry? Should you?

Pulling it all together: looking for strategic issues

Your strategic issues may emerge from any of the aspects we have spoken about so far. If you have undertaken a PESTEL analysis, you may wish to keep it in mind as you read on. Not only does the outside world of politics and economics sometimes move very rapidly, your more internal appreciation of your business and of your market will also mature. You may see new insights, and a PESTEL is a living document.

If, on the other hand, you have systematically looked at the general attractiveness of your industry using the Five Forces framework, then you now have a sketched insight into the competitive position of your organisation within that industry. Yet this is a partial picture only.

The final element in this chapter is the SWOT (strengths, weaknesses, opportunities and threats) matrix – see Figure 2.1. Everyone knows what a SWOT is, but few actually use it in the way it was originally intended when it was first proposed (in the late 1950s). A good SWOT analysis contrasts (i) things

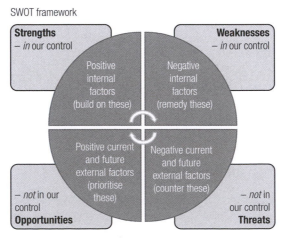

Figure 2.1 The SWOT framework

you have control over with things you do not and (ii) judgements on things that are working for you against things that are not. Out of all this comes strategic issue identification. Some have since reversed the order, creating a TOWS analysis that prioritises the external over the internal analysis, but the core idea remains the same.

A SWOT is usually a closing or summary of the situation and one of the final pieces of the puzzle before the identification of possible strategic issues. Once you have done that, you are ready to collect together your ideas for closer inspection.

 **tip**

A SWOT only collects relevant information and puts it in categories. On its own, this has no meaning. The analysis and the decisions must follow.

Doing strategy: where can you get your data from?

Remember, you are looking for strategic issues and so you will need to look beyond the day-to-day information you rely on to perform your job now. You are looking for information about cost structures, macroeconomic and regulatory trends, demographics and infrastructure details that will happen over the next 5, 10 or 20 years. Here is a list of sources of intelligence, all of which could inform your search:

● organisations and associations that specialise in your industry or in your geographical area (e.g. chambers of commerce);

● mainstream media and press, especially in specialist broadcasts on business topics, current affairs or economic analysis, industry reports produced by consulting firms;

- non-governmental organisations (NGOs), watchdog and consumer groups;
- regulatory bodies and their websites or publications, government and ministry information sources, business school research centres;
- networking groups, former colleagues (anyone you meet could be a potential source of data);
- supervisory board and executives within your organisation, functional heads of departments.

Once you have gathered data about the business environment, there needs to be a process to convert it into useful information for strategy planning. This may include internal workshops and awaydays devoted to working with the issues identified, and external input from consultants and organisation development experts. We will look at this aspect in more detail in later.

brilliant recap

In this chapter, these are the main things you can apply or bring to your own practice as a manager:

- You must know (or find out) what your organisation's reason is for being. What was its original purpose? What is its purpose now?

- The most important driver of strategy will be any issue that affects value creation.

- According to Michael Porter, there are two fundamental questions about which every organisation should be concerned: what are the factors that make your industry attractive enough to compete in and how best can you position yourself against your competitors?

> ● To identify your strategic issues, apart from asking whether yours is a good industry to be in, look at the growth curve of the industry and the life cycle of your organisation.
>
> The next question is often whether you are sufficiently different from your competition to become, and remain, profitable.

References

[1] If your management says it does not see any strategic issues, then that is its strategic issue.

[2] Greiner, L. (1972) 'Evolution and revolution as organizations grow', *Harvard Business Review*, July–August, pp. 37–46.

[3] Brewer, L. and Scott Hansen, M. (2004) *Confessions of an Enron Executive: A Whistleblower's Story*. Indiana: AuthorHouse, p. 31.

[4] http://www.campanemarinelli.com/en/ [accessed: 6 April 2015].

[5] https://www.startwithwhy.com/ for all you Sinekistas!

[6] 'Global Hotels & Motels Industry Profile' (2014) *Hotels & Motels Industry Profile: Global*, pp. 1–35, Business Source Complete, EBSCO-host Online Research Databases [accessed: 11 May 2015].

[7] Porter, M.E. (1985) *Competitive Strategy*. New York: Free Press.

CHAPTER 3

Strategic directions

Your equation isn't right. It isn't even wrong.

Wolfgang Paul

How this chapter will help you

Strategies create momentum and steer organisations in a particular direction. The larger the organisation, the more important it is to have thought carefully in advance about that direction. This chapter is about what kinds of choices you will need to make and what sorts of options are available to you.

Introduction

What direction should we take next? There are not many bigger questions than this in management. If an industry is attractive and worth competing in, then what methods should you use to create value there? For any organisation already operating in a competitive industry space, this means working out how to defend a position and/or open routes to expand into new areas. For any organisation not yet in what looks like a good business, strategic direction is about finding the best ways to enter.

 **tip**

Strategy is one part intuition in seeing what is coming, one part analysis in choosing what action to take and one part taking action. Don't forget, it is also one part chance.

Strategic decision making is not quite the same as the day-to-day activity that most managers undertake. Strategic issues can result from specific conditions or tensions inside an organisation but, generally, they emerge in the relationship between that and what is coming over the horizon in the world outside. Strategy is constantly looking out for and responding to changes in the long-term business environment. Amongst other things, this means:

- anticipating the expectations of important stakeholders;
- aligning to the expectations and intentions of the shareholders and founders;
- being open to changing the entire *scope* of what the organisation does, if necessary;
- making sure that the right *resources* are available, exactly where and when they are needed.

'What's the use of running if you're on the wrong road?'

German proverb

That is already quite a lot to have on your plate, but then you also have to deal with making strategic activity measurable. Strategic decisions may be forward looking, but they will affect everybody and everything in the organisation right now, so you need strong leadership skills, too.

you need strong leadership skills

Framing strategic choices

The business environment is ever-changing, complex and dynamic. For this reason, most strategists agree that, if you only carry on doing what you have done in the past, you may well find you have no future. But you will need courage to change what has been working well. Why? There are three main reasons:

1 **It is not easy to set a new direction:** you need a good way of generating options and choosing between them. There can seem to be so many different directions you *could* take, and so many possible strategies to get there, that the decision on what to do can be very difficult to pin down.

2 **There is a risk factor:** the new world you have in mind may have all sorts of its own hidden traps and unforeseen problems. In fact, you might not even succeed. Ken Blanchard, American management expert and author of the *One Minute Manager* books, estimates that up to 70 per cent of change initiatives fail.[1] The main problem, he says, concerns . . .

3 **People!** For both good and bad reasons, the people inside your organisation probably will not like the idea of change and may resist it. You may also grow through merger and acquisition, and bringing cultures together requires tact and skill. On the other hand, there is no strategy that can ever work without the enthusiasm and belief of those involved.

Later I will look in more detail at leadership of strategy, so let us begin with the first problem on the list above – generating choices. You will get into this best by first understanding the (theoretical) nature of competition.

What is competition?

Let us start with the three main types of competition recognised by economic theorists:

1 **Perfect competition:** a more or less theoretical situation in which existing buyers and sellers in a market have

complete access to information. Nothing is hidden, nothing is unknown, no one can sneak ahead of anyone else and it is impossible for anyone to influence prices, which are set as a margin above the cost of production (and not in regard to what others are charging). Price does not fall because demand is such that it would come down to only a point where newcomers or outsiders are prevented from entering the market. No one puts up their prices either, as this simply attracts new entrants for whom the market has suddenly become attractive. Perfect competition is mainly used as a concept by regulators of markets.

2 **Monopoly:** the opposite of perfect competition, and equally theoretical. A monopoly is where there is only one player who excludes all others to the point where price is set as they wish. In practice, only near-monopolies ever exist, and then very rarely and never for long. But the *idea* of a monopoly is important in deciding where the limits of legislation (and good taste) should be.

3 **Oligopoly:** far from theoretical – a version of this is reality for nearly every organisation. Here there is real competition between a few dominant players (there may be many smaller players, too, but they tend to follow, not lead). Usually, the bigger players are all about the same size and are involved in an interactive dance of leading and following strategy and tactics.

 **definition**

Competition

This describes the rivalry between companies that offer the same or similar offerings to the same or similar market segments.

Whatever your business or activity, even if you are working in the public or not-for-profit sectors, it is very unlikely that you are the only one in that space. More than anything, it is competition that drives strategic analysis and planning in a market where companies are trying to maximise value creation. In other words, you are bound to be very curious about what your rivals are up to. This is true even if you buy into the idea that strategy is warfare and success must be at the expense of any others in your space.

Assuming that all necessary legal, financial and social frameworks are in place, every enterprise needs two things. Everything else in business and in management flows from these fundamentals:

1   A customer with a need that can be met.
2   The resources and motivation to meet that need, profitably.

Statistically, the majority of new businesses fail. If a start-up survives the initial phase and grows to a size where it can measure its share of a market, it will, eventually, need to answer two more questions:

1   Is the overall market for what you make or do getting bigger or smaller?
2   Is your *share* of this existing market or industry getting bigger or smaller?

Figure 3.1 shows the four basic strategic permutations this presents.

As you can see, over time, products, services or even whole businesses will be in one of four basic positions. The whole market can grow, reduce or stay the same (and this may be cyclical) whilst, at the same time, your share of that market may also be growing, shrinking or staying flat. Knowing this information is not enough. You cannot judge where you are as

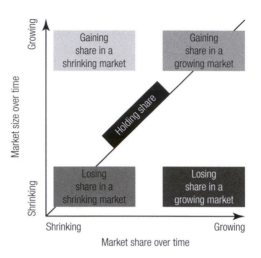

Figure 3.1 Market share/market growth matrix
Source: Adapted from The BCG Portfolio Matrix from the Product Portfolio Matrix, © 1970, The Boston Consulting Group (BCG).

good or bad unless you also consider the contextual factors we looked at earlier (alas, there are no absolutes and few simple answers in strategy). If everyone is leaving the business you are in, your share will go up in the short term, but is it sustainable? Should Boeing, for example, continue to make 747 jets in a world demanding smaller planes?

Executives have long looked to the relationship between growth and share as input into portfolio decisions. The Boston Consulting Group's famous growth–share matrix, which uses different metrics for its x and y axes from Figure 3.1 above, was the first. Developed over 40 years ago, the BCG matrix famously coined four labels, **dogs** (a falling share in a shrinking market), **cash cows** (an increasing share of a shrinking market), **stars** (a growing share of a growing market) and **question marks** or **problem children** (an unknown or small share of a growing market) and these terms have entered general management-speak, somewhat loosely. Rather than looking for easy shortcuts and convenient labels, it would be more useful to ask some hard questions about the future of your business as a whole.

Generic strategies

So what choices do you have? Once again, the name of Michael Porter has dominated the debate here. Enter the concept of the generic strategy.

 **question**

Sometimes the imagination of senior management does not match the reality of the one the organisation has in place. Is your organisation able to carry out its own strategic plans?

Porter believes that analysing your competitive position is the key to success and that certain sorts of definite action can be taken to protect, defend or grow a position in a market or in an industry. This is based on the

analysing your competitive position is the key to success

notion that the context of your strategic issue is a problem of economic competition and that a generic strategy is a tool to start the job. This, at least, has the virtue of making a decision easy, because there are only a limited number of options available to you. Three ways, actually. According to Porter, an organisation can excel over its rivals (via analysis of the Five Forces influencing the industry environment) through:

● cost leadership;
● differentiation;
● focus.

Cost leadership

When customers care about the price most, cost leadership is the determined effort to create and then maintain an advantage over competitors by careful control of spending in any area that delivers value to a customer. The organisation's whole strategy must reflect this in order to get a higher return than its competitors. It may also deter new entrants, whose costs are likely to be higher.

Cost leadership often correlates to market share, economies of scale, capital investment, specialised skills in processes and operations, influence over your supply chain, a culture of reports and controls and a leadership that rewards managers for meeting strict cost and budget targets. These also constitute barriers to entry for others.

Differentiation

When customers are willing to pay a premium price for something they value (such as performance, quality or reputation), then differentiation is a strategy where you create a product or service that others in your industry (sadly, it is not enough only for your CEO to think this) acknowledge is unique or, at least, very hard to copy. Porter notes that differentiation may not produce high market share and can be expensive to achieve.

Differentiation requires skills to develop and market new and innovative products and services. You also must have good communication with sales or distribution channels, a culture of coordination and creativity amongst the various departments and functions, and leadership to attract and inspire people with valuable skills. Again, these double up as barriers to entry.

Focus

When customers in a *particular* market or segment are identified as key, then focus is the concentration of either cost leadership or differentiation to that one particular segment, product or geographic region. The idea is to aim at better than average returns in *that* area. Focus, you will not be surprised to hear, is narrow and may not match the strategy the company is taking overall in its industry.

Porter's logic was that if you fail to achieve (or follow) these, then you will be 'stuck in the middle'. When that happens, it is essential to act to modernise and to re-position yourself in your market, which you do by analysing certain aspects of your market, your business or your industry. A generic strategy will need refinement, but is handy – if only because the labels have become quite well known and make it slightly easier to communicate strategic intent from the top down – which is part of minimising resistance when implementing change in an organisation. I am not sure that is such a positive psychology to follow – surely your staff are smarter than that – nor such a realistic one. Many businesses find they need to use a combination of approaches that do not sit neatly in Porter's categories.

Take a look at this example below.

 **example**

Lethabo maize milling, South Africa[2]

Many of the products consumers enjoy daily have their origins in corn: jams, jellies, sauces, marinades, cereals, condiments, tinned fruits and vegetables, baked goods, meat products like bolognese and hot dogs, yoghurts, snack items, cough drops, antibiotics, intravenous solutions, toothpaste, paper, cosmetics and soap, to name a few.

In many subsistence agricultural societies, maize (also referred to as corn) has long been the key crop for feeding people and livestock. Fuelled by population growth and advances in farming methods and industrial applications of the starches and sugars in maize, an amazing array of products based on maize production, milling and refining are now used in a wide variety of products and process. Corn starches are used in many foods and beverages, in laundry care products and adhesives, in packaging, plastics, textiles and also for bio-fuels. For many of us, it would be virtually ▶

impossible to get through a day without (knowingly or unknowingly) using a product sourced, in part, from maize.

Globally, maize milling and refining is big business; the so-called ABCD conglomerates of Archer Daniels Midland, Bunge, Cargill and Louis Dreyfus control 90 per cent of the global market in commodities such as maize. Global production in 2013 was a staggering 1 billion tonnes, of which only 71.6 million was grown in Africa. In South Africa, maize production for that year was 1.24 million tonnes.[3] Maize is a staple part of the South African diet and is used for livestock feed. Pap, coarsely-ground maize flour, is the anchor in much local cuisine.

Until recently, milling and retail had been dominated by foreign-owned producers and brands. Set up in 2014 by its CEO Xolani Ndzaba, who grew up in Soweto, Lethabo (which means joy in the Sesotho language) is the first black-owned enterprise in this sector. With £500,000 in loans and investment from ABSA bank and local retailer Massmart, Lethabo Milling wants to challenge the grip of the bigger brands in South Africa: Iwisa (a brand of Premier, which is owned by Luxembourg-listed investors Brait), Ace (part of Tiger Brands) and White Star (Pioneer Foods). Ndzaba's mill can produce 36,000 tonnes a year and, annually, is supplying Massmart with 10,000 tonnes for its own-label brand, as well as a Lethabo-branded product. This support ensures that Lethabo can be part of the concerted effort to support local SMEs in supply-chain development. By global standards, the new venture might not be big but, after several years of lack of funding for Ndzaba, the support means he can grow the business into a profitable and sustainable entity.

How would you describe the strategy being used by Lethabo Milling? From what you know, and remembering the special conditions in South Africa, what do you think of its competitive position? What advice would you give Xolani as he tries to establish and grow his business? Although only in its early stages, what do you think Lethabo Milling should keep in mind as it develops?

Michael Porter's insights were fresh and logical when they first appeared and many large organisations were able to build some elements of his definition of competitive advantage into their planning and operations. But, when you apply a theory, you also accept its assumptions about the way markets work. Remember:

● how we see the nature of competitive and profit-driven industries is always changing; the past is predictable, but the future does not always follow on from how things were;

● in many parts of the world, new industries and new or emerging economies are developing their own models and measurements of value.

What other choices are there to grow?

Strategists are born worriers. They are always afraid of missing what everyone is seeing and of failing to capitalise (strike whilst the iron is hot) on what is coming up. It should be no surprise, then, to find that there is no shortage of other views and advice on strategic direction.

> **strategists are born worriers**

brilliant tip

'Do nothing' is a strategic option you should always calculate. When considering change, always make sure you include this possibility – even if only as a comparison to use with other ideas.

Igor Ansoff, a thought-leader in strategy in the 1950s and 1960s, developed what has become a popular matrix to guide senior managers.[4] The main choices are between existing or new products, and existing or new markets, as in Figure 3.2. These produce four growth strategies, which are outlined below:

| Existing markets/ existing products
Market penetration | Existing markets/ new products
Product development |
| New markets/ existing products
Market development | New markets/ new products
Diversification |

Figure 3.2 Ansoff's diversification matrix
Source: Ansoff, I. (1957) 'Strategies for diversification', *Harvard Business Review* 35(5), September–October, pp. 113–124. Reprinted by permission of *Harvard Business Review*. Copyright © 1957 by the Harvard Business School Publishing Corporation, all rights reserved.

Market penetration

Market penetration means finding new customers in your existing market, either by taking share from a competitor or, perhaps, by buying up one of your rivals and taking theirs. Better promotion or access to new channels and various tactics with pricing can also produce growth in this way.

Market development

If you have products or services that are going great guns, you may decide that the best way to grow is by introducing them to new customers (grow your market). There are various options for how this may be done, which can include new locations or territories (e.g. export, licensing, joint venture, etc.) or even identifying a brand new segment. A classic example of this was the mouthwash Listerine, which originally was developed as an antiseptic liquid for use in hospitals and for cleaning floors. In the 1920s it was repositioned as an oral cure for bad breath, and sales took off!

Product development

The alternative to finding a new market is finding new products to sell to a market you know. Selling something new to people who already know what you do may be a very logical plan. Extending a product line is often the signal that you have arrived. If people trust you, you can tap into their natural curiosity for novelty. This strategy usually calls for research and development, so can be expensive, but many companies will use acquisition or merger to achieve the same effect. US pharmaceutical giant Pfizer's repeated and (as yet) unsuccessful attempts to buy UK-Swedish rival Astra Zeneca may be an example of this. Alternative tactics for this include becoming the licensee for someone else's product or some form of joint cooperation.

Diversification

Diversification means moving into both new markets and new products at the same time. There are actually two types of diversification. In the first, the organisation develops a portfolio of businesses or products that may be completely unrelated to each other. A very successful exponent of this is Warren Buffett's Berkshire Hathaway, a holding company that owns an enormous range of businesses. The second route is more conventional and combines the product and market development strategies above. When a firm has grown beyond its original (single) activity, it becomes a multi-business organisation. Alternatively, it may diversify by moving up or down its own supply chain (this is called vertical integration).

Strategists *love* talking about the last of these, diversification. Even though many companies will not reach a size or a success where they will diversify, the underlying principles are worth understanding. There are two reasons for this. First, many successful and growing companies become even bigger and even more successful by buying up single-business firms (in other words, *you* could end up being part of someone else's diversification strategy). Second, many business and management lessons are available to you by studying how other businesses diversify.

There are two further considerations for direction in diversification:

1 **Route:** when a decision to diversify is made in a single unit business, how is this to be done? For example, do you set something up *organically from the inside* by setting up a new business yourself from scratch, or do you *buy it in from outside* by acquiring an existing going concern? Alternatively, do you create a partnership with another company and develop something jointly? Or do you enlarge the business by moving up or down the supply chain?

The latter of these is what Spanish fashion retailer company Zara has done. It manufactures more than half of its own clothes in its own factories (shortening lead times on new lines). The alternative is to outsource.

 **definition**

Outsourcing

This is hiring others to do something your organisation has previously done itself. The formal transfer via contract to a third party of an internally organised activity is now big business globally, but usually is restricted to non-core activities.

2 **Scope:** the bigger the enterprise, the more components there are to be managed. In very large organisations, strategic activity is built around **strategic business units**

(SBUs), which give parts of a business freedom to move ahead in their own environment in their own way, without the need to have decisions approved from above. This is one example of how strategy affects the work of managers at the business level, as we will see in Part 2.

Strategic decisions can be made to reduce scope as well as let it grow. In addition, the various units of a business may not all be of the same size or importance and you may not distribute your energy or your strategic planning equally everywhere. The tension between centralisation and decentralisation affects everyone who leads or implements strategy.

Route and scope may overlap in strategic direction, but diversification is often very difficult to achieve through organic growth. You might be big enough to move into a new business area, but do you have the know-how, or the resources, without damaging your core business? Also, you do not, usually, have the economies of scale of existing players in the new area, making the payback period much longer.

There are two main choices open to an organisation that wishes to expand into pastures new:

- mergers and acquisitions;
- strategic alliances.

Mergers and acquisitions

These happen all the time and, globally, deals amount to about $2 trillion every year.[5] Mega-takeovers fill the news pages (as for example, in August 2015 when Nikkei paid £844 million for the *Financial Times* from Pearson), but the vast majority are on a much smaller scale. Many entrepreneurs will look to acquisition as their preferred exit strategy, and many investors see attractive returns as an alternative to other forms of investment.

For companies looking for market share to create value, mergers or acquisitions are an easy way to achieve it. Other reasons may be more defensive, such as preventing a rival getting access. Mergers and acquisitions (M & A) can be *same-sector* or *different-sector*. *Same-sector* deals lead to dominant market share, economies of scale, shared expertise and stronger bargaining power with suppliers and buyers. *Different-sector* M & A activity is either *vertical* integration or *horizontal* integration. Vertical means moving *upstream* into direct and indirect suppliers or *downstream* to those who were previously your customers.

 **tip**

Too much same-sector M & A can actually *increase* competition, as new entrants now perceive the possibility to enter a less crowded market with an innovation.

Horizontal growth deals move you sideways from your core activity into closely or distantly related businesses.

The most active sectors for mergers and acquisitions in the coming few years are likely to be in the healthcare/pharmaceutical industry, closely followed by media and telecoms. Company acquisitions can be complex and long drawn-out affairs, and there is no guarantee that a deal will go through. Mergers can also be difficult as systems struggle to integrate. Even my own area, Higher Education, is not immune. A few years ago, the management school where I work merged with a major university to form a new business school (one of several examples in the sector). Estimates vary, but approximately 70–80 per cent of deals fail to realise their original potential. For this reason, a less committed route to value creation via collaboration is a very common strategy: strategic alliances.

Strategic alliances

They can move in the same vertical and horizontal directions as mergers and acquisitions, but give more flexibility and carry less risk. An alliance lets you put your toe in the water to test a new market without committing your equity or capital investment. If it goes wrong, you can withdraw, and if it goes well, you can invest further. Horizontal alliances (selective cooperation with competitors) can be used to defend against a much more dominant player, or to share what otherwise would be very expensive technology or resources.

The word synergy should be used here because often an alliance helps cut out duplication or reduce risk for new investment. A formal type of strategic alliance is the **joint venture** (JV), in which both sides tie up some equity in order to achieve a given strategic objective together. JVs can also be a prelude to merger, a sort of trial arrangement to see whether a more involved agreement would work. This is how Sony Mobile came into existence in 2012 as a wholly owned subsidiary of Sony in Japan, following a nine-year JV with Sweden's mobile phone manufacturer, Ericsson. To work, all such JVs call for openness and trust, but this can be difficult to achieve since it is rare for both partners to be equal or to have equally open cultures.

brilliant tip

Before considering an alliance consider the history, culture and purpose (including values) of the prospective partner.

In 2014 a survey of American mergers and acquisitions by the consulting firm KPMG revealed that the top five intentions for the following year were:

- Opportunistic – target becomes available   21%
- Expand geographic reach   19%
- Expand customer base   16%
- Enter into new lines of business   15%
- Financial buyer looking for profitable
  operations and/or gain on exit   11%[6]

But activity of this kind does not always work out and the direction of flow can go the other way through divestment (and, remember, one firm's divestment is another's growth).

 **example**

Tesco divests[7]

The UK mobile industry may have just four major networks, but this supports a market with around 100 branded services that use this infrastructure. The largest of these non-network providers is Tesco Mobile, with 4 million customers. Tesco Mobile is a joint venture between the giant British retailer and O2, and is estimated to be worth about £100 million a year in profits to each.

In May 2015 the *Guardian* reported that Tesco was preparing the way to sell its mobile business. This news came hot on the heels of a series of recent divestments by Tesco. In January 2015, it sold its TV video streaming service Blinkbox Music to TalkTalk for £5 million, in a deal that included Tesco's 75,000 broadband and 20,000 landline customers, and Blinkbox Books looks set to follow. In June 2015 Tesco started to prepare the way for the sale of Dunnhumby, the company that created Tesco's innovative Clubcard loyalty scheme in 1989. Estimates of the value of Dunnhumby to a buyer began at £2 billion, but, by August, the *Financial Times* was reporting this as having been cut to £700 million, which put even more pressure on Tesco in its plans to sell its South Korean retail business, Homeplus.

All these actions follow a series of recent poor trading results in the UK and abroad, as well as several embarrassing accounting scandals that included a £250 million overstatement of half-yearly profits in 2014. New CEO Dave Lewis has vowed to turn this around but Tesco needs to raise at least £5 billion to redress a £22 billion debt hole in its balance sheet.

As the *Financial Times* reported in May, 'The value of Tesco Mobile will in part be the brand itself, although the retailer operates more than 250 Tesco Phone shops. Tesco also sells as many as two million mobile phones a year. Tesco operates a value-based mobile service, which has a number of direct rivals such as TalkTalk and GiffGaff.'[8]

These are tough times for Tesco PLC. In April 2015, it was forced to announce a £6.4 billion pre-tax loss in its 2014 accounts and, in every business in which it operates, it does so under intense competition. Grocery retailing in the UK is one of the most competitive markets in the world, and the once mighty Tesco is being squeezed between discount retailers, such as Aldi or Lidl, and high-end providers, such as Marks & Spencer or Waitrose. Long gone are the ambitious plans for more out-of-town superstores, and the fleet of corporate jets has been sold off.

How many of the different types of strategic direction so far described can you spot echoing in the Tesco story? What do you think Tesco should do next?

Putting it all together

In his 1982 book, *The Mind of the Strategist,* McKinsey management expert Kenichi Ohmae foresaw many of the themes in this chapter.[9] He envisaged a strategic triangle of *customer, competitor* and *corporation* (you). There are, he said, three routes to competitive advantage:

1 **Reallocate resources,** but stick only to your most basic success factors.

2 **Focus on exploiting one's relative strength.** This means analysing your competitor's strengths and weaknesses and

then acting on a feature where they are not strong but you could be.

3 **Redefine the strategic issue of the business by taking a bold action.** Question the orthodox way of doing things in your business. Asking 'why?' continuously might sound annoying, but is what can lead to big breakthroughs.

> it is the duty of a manager to exploit any opportunity

It is the duty of a manager to exploit any opportunity that will grow the value of the firm and help it reach its purpose. Sometimes the growth and financial return aspect is at the forefront, but, in some sectors, the purpose (which may be an intangible social benefit) should dominate.

I should add here that you will find a number of these ideas challenged later on. The terrain of management is not this clear-cut, and the boundary between what the duty of a manager is and the unspoken assumptions behind what is right and what is wrong (in business at least) need to be brought to light.

 **recap**

Here is a summary of the main ideas that you can apply or bring to your own practice as a manager:

- Strategy deals with competitive threats and evaluates and exploits opportunities.

- Strategic direction answers the question 'What shall we be competitive in?'

- All strategic activity is intended to create value. Three broad criteria for judging the value of a new strategic direction include:
    - Will it increase quality?
    - Will it increase productivity?
    - Will it release cash?

> Future impact is the most obvious indicator of what makes any decision strategic rather than tactical or operational.
>
> These mean that very careful consideration of all aspects of the decisions you make at corporate level is needed. Get it right and you can ensure the future survival of your company. Get it wrong and literally everything may be at stake.

References

[1] Blanchard, K. (2010) 'Mastering the Art of Change', *The Training Journal.* Available from: www.kenblanchard.com

[2] http://lethabomilling.co.za/

[3] Food and Agricultural Organisation (FAO) statistics.

[4] Ansoff, I. (1957) 'Strategies for diversification', *Harvard Business Review* 35(5), September–October, pp. 113–124.

[5] https://hbr.org/2011/03/the-big-idea-the-new-ma-playbook

[6] Nachman, S. (2014) 'The Boom is Back: M&A Re-emerges as Leading Growth Strategy', *2015 M&A Outlook Survey Report.* Available from: www.kpmg.com

[7] Compiled by the author. Sources include various 2015 news stories in the *Guardian* and the *Financial Times.* For example, see http://www.theguardian.com/business/2015/may/08/tesco-mobile-sale-debt-o2

[8] http://www.ft.com/fastft/320541/tesco-sell-mobile-business

[9] Ohmae, K. (1982) *The Mind of the Strategist: The Art of Japanese Business.* New York: McGraw-Hill.

PART 2

Business level strategy

Experience is the name everyone gives to their mistakes.

Oscar Wilde

S trategy takes the long view about the direction of an organisation. At the corporate level, the owners/founders or their appointed representatives are making choices about what markets, in what mix and by what means they can best create value. CEOs are bound by an obligation to act in the interests of the owners above their own. This is known as **fiduciary duty.** Senior managers deal with a relatively small number of issues that require big decisions. However, it would be a mistake to believe that strategy is finished with as soon as corporate decisions have been made. It is one thing to set a compelling goal in line with the purpose and vision of the organisation, but quite another to follow it through. For that, you require the right people, enough investment and the correct processes. The hard work is starting.

In smaller companies, the distance from top to bottom is usually a short one. Large organisations have added layers of complexity. To keep agile, they may have **strategic business units** (SBUs) that are able to plan and operate autonomously from each other. SBUs have their own competitive strategy and management teams and may be numerous (the Virgin Group, for example, has 7 SBUs, while GE has 49).[1]

Part 2 of *Brilliant Strategy for Business* is about the delivery end of strategy; the nitty-gritty details. This is the part of the book that addresses what happens amidst the messy reality of the present, where things do not always go to plan. To be a brilliant business strategist at this level you need:

- the ability to make *informed* strategic choices to guide the business unit in the right direction and plan for change; remember, this is the engine room where value is actually created;
- management skills to evaluate how things are progressing; in larger businesses, often it is difficult to see the wood for the trees and, even in medium to small size companies, implementing a strategy requires a lot of coordination;
- leadership skills to inspire – this is critical: when it comes to strategy, every manager must also be prepared to be a leader.

I am going to begin with what is probably the most dominant idea in strategy analysis – competitive advantage (Chapter 4). Finding it and keeping it has become the primary aim in stable industries and in predictable markets. But we live in unpredictable and fast-changing times, so a challenge to this view has emerged with the idea of the learning organisation and the concept of disruptive innovation (Chapter 5). Wherever your emphasis, an organisation's strategy will, eventually, affect all parts of a business (including yours), so it is important to understand how every core function has a strategic aspect (Chapter 6). Strategy and leadership have long been linked, though the relationship is complex because leadership can mean different things to different people. What people actually do (or should do) when they implement strategy is therefore the final word in this part of the book (Chapter 7).

Reference

[1] The advantages of a portfolio of SBUs are that they help manage (i) the balance of the business investment, (ii) cash flows and (iii) flexibility of market conditions in different sectors. The disadvantages include (i) difficult to coordinate and analyse when there are too many, (ii) conflicts of interest are possible between them and, conversely, (iii) synergies can be lost when some are divested.

CHAPTER 4

Finding competitive advantage

My formula for success is rise early, work late, and strike oil.

Paul Getty

How this chapter will help you

If you were the *only* ones doing what you do, you would have a monopoly. Strategy, quite frankly, would be a fairly dull subject for you. Luckily, you are surrounded by other businesses and other organisations, each with its own aims, objectives and talents, so your life is more interesting. And complex. Your customer has a choice and you have your limitations on what you can feasibly do. This chapter will help you identify what is special about you and what you do.

Introduction

Judging by the number of books on the subject, competitive advantage may be easier to talk about than achieve.

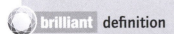 **brilliant** definition

Competitive advantage

This is the strategy of achieving your goals by getting and staying ahead of your rivals in a given market. It is often defined as sustaining higher than average profits compared to rivals.

If you work in a for-profit organisation, you will agree (or your boss will) that consistently achieving above-average returns for your industry would be a great goal to have; particularly if you can do this despite the best efforts of your competitors to stop you. This chapter presents two related perspectives on how to achieve it:

1 **From the outside in:** management responds to the changing demands of the environment by analysing the optimum *position* against competitors in a chosen market.

2 **From the inside out:** management builds on the right internal *resources* and *competences* to prepare for the future by identifying unique strengths, talents and capabilities it has or can get.

Positioning and *resourcing* might appear unconnected, but these approaches are often used in conjunction with each other. The lure of competitive advantage is that it is adaptable and applicable at every level in the organisation:

● at the top, *headquarters* must think about long-term vision and corporate planning, investment and the best interests of the shareholders;

● *strategic business units* (SBUs) must consider not only how medium-term decisions will affect the competitive position in their part of the organisation but also how they align with overall corporate aims;

● *strategic planning units* (SPUs) must implement the various decisions made above them while also paying attention to the competitive position of the particular groups of products or service lines they run;

● *individual product or service lines* (brands), the smallest unit of competitive positioning, must compete in their own market niches and still somehow remain aligned with *all* the levels above.

What actually counts as a competitive advantage is very elusive, however. To see why, bear in mind five questions:

1 **Who?** Defining with whom you are competing (and with whom you are not) is an important component of this approach. The bedrock of competitive advantage is outperformance of rivals over time. Blockbuster, for example, once led the way in VHS and then DVD film rentals, but failed to recognise that its real competition was online.

2 **Where?** Proximity often plays a part in a firm's competitive position. This may be geographical clusters (e.g. Silicon Valley, the City of London) where similar businesses co-locate to benefit from, for example, market access, business intelligence or economies of scale, or networks where companies deliberately reach out to create ties over a distance.[1] These can create a strategic advantage.

3 **How?** Getting ahead implies action. How good and how complete is your information? How complete does it need to be? How will you stop yourself from managing only in response to what your competitors are doing, perhaps missing the bigger picture of what is going on away from that?

4 **What?** Staying ahead implies measurement. What are you going to measure your success against? Have you got the resources in place to create the change that will create value in the future?

5 **Why?** Is *everything* dictated by your position against your competition? You need to check any dangerous assumptions you might be making about your goals. Have you lost sight of your customers in the battle with your rivals? Are there customers you have not met yet?

Another phrase that helps define competitive advantage is a company's **unique competing space,** which is the combination of three major schools of thought in strategy.

brilliant definition

Unique competing space

This is a conceptual place for value creation formed in the crossover points of three boundaries:

1   Customer needs (that must be identified).

2   Competitor offerings (that do not yet reach this need).

3   Available resources.

If you can *mobilise resources* that fulfil a *customer's needs* in a way that *competitors cannot* (yet), then you have the basis of a viable strategy.[2]

This allows an assessment of new initiatives in strategic business units and it assumes three things:

● There would be economic returns higher than for most of your competitors.

● You truly understand what your customer and other stakeholders want that is not currently available.

● Your organisation has relevant capabilities and can learn, change and innovate.

As a strategist, your task is to be clear about these different sources of competitive advantage. So let us look at them from the two most common angles – outside-in, and inside-out.

From the outside in

Competitive advantage comes from those value-creating elements that you possess but others do not. This is sometimes called the **value proposition,** and is your best explanation as to why a customer should buy from you and not from a competitor. Michael Porter has built a powerful argument that there are two main sources of competitive advantage: price advantage and cost advantage.

Price advantage

This is where you possess, or your product/service does, features that are worth enough to a customer to deserve a premium paid for them (we can call these benefits). The best sources are benefits that others cannot easily replicate, imitate or substitute.

 **example**

Claridge's

Claridge's is a five-star luxury hotel in London's Mayfair and it has a unique value proposition. A part of the exclusive Savoy Group, the hotel commands a price premium that is not so much based on its opulent décor and fine food, but the high standards of personal service. Staff profile their guests and retain knowledge of their preferences (even down to where they like the fixtures and fittings in the room arranged). Its Central London location and cachet of opulence and A-list guests certainly help. Any of these elements would be hard to copy and expensive to scale up. Guests in their market segment are happy to pay a high-price premium to stay at Claridge's because there is no one else who can offer quite the same personal attention to detail, which is what they value. This is an example of how one business achieves advantage through focused excellence in a service.

Most organisations using price advantage cannot score as strongly as Claridge's on all fronts. Can you think of any examples of companies you know that are able to charge a bit more – just because it is them? What elements do they rely on to constitute premium value? Simply being able to charge more is not always enough for a sustainable price advantage. If what it costs you to achieve or maintain your premium price is a lot higher than your competitors, you can become susceptible to losing share of your market.

Cost advantage

Cost advantage may be achieved when you can produce something to scale, thus making big savings on fixed costs as well as variable ones. The most obvious examples are in those sectors where low-value-add production can be moved to low-cost economies, or when there is access to an asset that others do not have (e.g. technology and patents). Cost advantage may also come from achieving much better levels of productivity than your competitors, and here is where strategy textbooks often start to tell the story of how the Japanese automotive and electronics industries conquered the United States.[3]

Sources of advantage over your competition vary, but often include the following:

● Having control over price. In other words, you can either charge your customer what you like, or you can deliver whatever price your customer likes and still make a profit.

---

brilliant example

If your customer is a member of the super-rich, then you can 'name your price'. This means you have a product or service that is rare, or valued, and you can be trusted to deliver to a very demanding specification. Italian luxury yacht builder Benetti safely falls into this category.[4]

At the other end of the spectrum, in 2007 British musicians Radiohead released an album with a variation on *trust-based pricing*. Listeners could download and *then* pay whatever price they thought it was worth (even zero).

● Product or service features protected by patent or copyright.

 **example**

Research and development is key for many companies to retain an edge over rivals. For 21 consecutive years, IBM has topped the charts for US patents received annually, successfully registering 6,809 protected ideas in 2013 alone. Interestingly, most of these are for software – a contrast to the company's former dominance of computer hardware and an indicator that sustained market advantage is not necessarily a matter of what you were once good at.

● Channels of distribution you own or to which you have exclusive access.

brilliant example

There are many e-book readers available on the market but, because it already has such a strong presence in online retailing, Amazon's Kindle e-reader has retained the dominant position in the market, providing an easy platform to download and read in excess of 3 million book titles.

● Consistently better levels of quality and service than others.

brilliant example

You may never have heard of Flextronics, but it is the world's second largest electronics manufacturing services (EMS) company, employing over 200,000 people in 30 countries. It supplies component parts and services to many household-name original equipment manufacturers (OEMs), such as Ford, Huawei and Apple. Success can be possible in such partnerships only when suppliers consistently meet demanding quality targets.

Do not forget that there may be other ways of achieving your organisation's purpose that do not quite fit these descriptions. If you are a non-profit organisation, you may be serving a mission that is achieved without consideration of a unique competing space; you may be more concerned about having a positive and long-term effect on the world around you than whether you are making this month's sales figures. But, even the best charity knows that it needs to fund its activities and that sources of money are scarce and the needs of other charities are equally pressing. Half an eye is always on finding better ways to achieve goals.

> half an eye is always on finding better ways to achieve goals

The Strategy Clock

Remember Porter's Generic Strategies? He gave us four basic options. The Strategy Clock, shown in Figure 4.1, was developed by British academics Cliff Bowman and David Faulkner in the 1990s.[5] They extended this to eight, chosen depending on how value is perceived by the customers, versus positioning with high or low prices.

The eight positions are:

1 **No frills:** no one is expecting any added value, so price is the only consideration.
2 **Low price:** in short, an attractive price.
3 **Hybrid:** seen by customers as a bargain, a low price is attached to a product with some perception of quality.
4 **Differentiation:** some feature of the product or service is used to justify a slightly higher price.

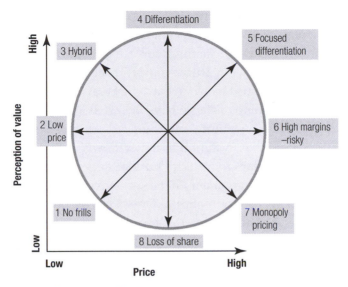

Figure 4.1 The Strategy Clock
Source: Johnson, G., Scholes, K. and Whittington, R. (2005) *Exploring Corporate Strategy*. 7th Ed. Harlow: FT Prentice Hall.

5 **Focused differentiation:** definitive perception of value from the unique features of a product or service means you can charge a premium price.

6 **High margins:** charging a high premium price for something that is not perceived as having any special feature is a risky strategy, since it leaves you open to competition on price (usually possible only in special circumstances).

7 **Monopoly pricing:** rarely found in anything other than the very short term and generally not scalable for long (exceptions are very specific, such as sales of bottled water in the departures area of a small airport).

8 **Loss of share:** not really a strategy, more a description for any product reaching obsolescence or end of life cycle, unable to command the price it once did. The stuff you cannot shift any more.

If you want to see evidence of the clock in action, visit the confectionery aisle of a large supermarket. Look it up and down. You will find (near the floor, almost out of sight) the own-brand bars (1. No frills), simply packaged and suspiciously cheap, compared to what will be at eye level – the most popular brands. These have invested more in image and ingredients (3. Hybrid), and there will be some on special offer (2. Low price) in the hope that you will switch or buy in bulk. Not too far from these, but not quite in prime location, are brands that you may have seen advertised but rarely see on offer (4. Differentiation). These rely on your loyalty. And, on the top shelf, come the expensive, specialist brands or niche bars (5. Focused differentiation) that rely partly on a price difference to appeal to particular consumers (organic chocolate, hand-made or sourced from single locations, and so on). You are very unlikely to see anything on sale in 6 (High margins) because who wants to pay a premium for ordinary chocolate?

Notice how the creation of categories for different types of strategic positioning in an industry allows various players to exploit their niche. The various brands, and their competing parent companies, rely on each other for their value proposition. This shows how positioning is relational; it also means, by the way, that innovation has boundaries – but more of that later.

brands rely on each other for their value proposition

Managers in many organisations seek this sort of stability, though they must remind themselves to look out for strategic drift over time. However, later in the book you will see how this idea of predictability in strategy is challenged by other strategists.

 **questions**

How did your organisation make its entry to the industry, market segment or product/service area it currently occupies? Do you see one or more of the routes from the Strategy Clock present in your organisation's positioning?

Porter's Value Chain framework

Porter's next contribution to strategy in this area comes in the form of the value chain – see Figure 4.2. The idea is ingenious – an easy and convenient way to measure the ability of your organisation to deliver consistently on its value proposition. The value chain applies common sense to look for strategic relevance. That is, finding where you can do things more cheaply or more productively than your competitors is dependent on making sure that all:

- **primary activities** (the chain of processes that *directly* transform your inputs into your distinctive outputs) can be measured to show their contribution to margin;

- **secondary activities** (the ones that allow all your primary activities to happen) can demonstrate their ability to achieve the chosen *strategic intent* of the primary activities.

The exact configuration of primary activities will vary from industry to industry and by type of organisation (and as it grows over time), but using this framework to analyse your business can reveal, for instance, where you are over- or under-spending on direct or indirect operational costs, or where you have fixed assets tied up in the business in a useful way and where you do not.

The Value Chain is not an organisational chart (although some companies have adopted it as such) but rather a lens to

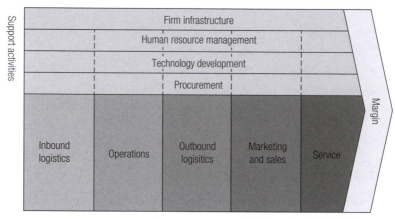

examine everything that goes on inside your organisation to see whether directly or indirectly it contributes to the margin (which is the difference between what it costs you to make or do something and the price a buyer is willing to pay you for it).

 **tip**

The value chain of your organisation is part of a whole industry **value system** that includes the value chains of your suppliers and buyers.

Let us pause for a moment.

So far, the formula for creating a competitive strategy seems to be:

1   Find a need. Then work out if meeting that need would – all other things being equal – be an attractive proposition financially (as well as ethically).

2   Find your competing space amongst all the other suppliers of that need. Look for the gaps and design a structure for your organisation to exploit them.

3   Concentrate most of your efforts on outwitting your rivals, rather like in a game of chess.

4   Grow by choosing and pursuing one of a limited set of generic strategies.

Is this enough for *sustained* competitive advantage? No, say some strategists. They see a couple of problems with this outside-in philosophy. First, every organisation grows in a different way and, rather like people, they develop personalities and have unique talents. Trying to imitate what another organisation does well will not work because, even when the external conditions are the same, successful companies have something about them that unsuccessful companies do not. Second, this economic analysis of industry attractiveness is too static and backward-looking. The past is hardly a good predictor of the future. They may have a point. Everyone trying to be just like everyone else eventually leads to stagnation, and trying to predict the future when the business environment is becoming less and less stable can be a waste of time and money.

> every organisation grows in a different way

An alternative is to shift attention to what you have inside the organisation – and look for advantage there.

Inside out: resources and capabilities

The **resource-based view** (RBV) is the inside-out way of looking at competitive advantage, made popular following an article in 1990 by Gary Hamel and C.K. Prahalad in *Harvard Business Review* (though the idea of finding advantage from capabilities has been around since the 1950s). Companies, they said, should look at bundles of assets at their disposal in order to prepare for the future. This often starts with the question 'What business are we in?'

 **questions**

What business are you in? This may seem obvious, but there are parts of your business you would change or give up, if you needed to. What could you never stop doing?

What business you are in may be taken for granted. But, if you know what – at your core – you are about, then you might well ask, 'How are we competent at this in a way that others are not?' A competence – or competency – is the skill in doing something well, and is an aggregate or collection of intangible factors that include accumulated learning and experience.

 **definition**

Core competency

This is 'a harmonized combination of multiple resources and skills that distinguish a firm in the marketplace'.[6]

There are three key tests to identify the type that contribute to competitive advantage:

1 Does this capability (or could it, if developed) create customer value?

2 Does it (or would this) differentiate us from our competitors?

3 Will this competence generate new ideas? Can it be extended?

Having introduced the world to the idea of the core competence, Hamel and Prahalad say that the competition that really matters is not the one for products or services, but for the assets and resources that can generate these in the future; a subtle difference, but an important one. A valuable strategic resource or asset should:

● be impossible or very difficult for anyone else to copy or do as well as you;

● be difficult to substitute with something else;

● have a long-lasting positive benefit;

● not be embodied in your staff or customers, either of which may leave you. So, a good CEO is not a valuable strategic asset (try telling some of them this!) and neither is your main customer.

If you can identify key resources that tick all these boxes, then the theory says you should organise everything you do around them.

> a good CEO is not a valuable strategic asset

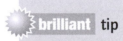 **brilliant** tip

Identify what valuable strategic resources your current organisation has.

VRIO

Resource-based strategy builds from your base and looks for alternatives that others cannot copy. How do you get them? And how should you assess your strategic resources in terms of your value proposition? One way of doing this is with a framework called VRIO, which asks the following Yes/No questions:

- **Does it have value creation potential?** This is the litmus test. There might be a lot of things that are distinctive about your organisation, but can they make any difference to the bottom line? Can they be exploited? Can you prevent others getting them?

- **Is it rare?** Scarcity is a fundamental driver of value in economic theory. This is anything you have that is either intrinsically difficult to find (e.g. it is scarce in nature), or that only you have gained sole access to or control of (e.g. it is the result of years of accumulated experience or knowledge).

- **Is it hard to imitate?** On the TV show *Dragon's Den* you often see great ideas pitched to the wealthy investors being rejected for investment purely on the basis that they would be too easy for others to copy. Anything that you have that is distinctive, commercial and expensive to imitate is a source of value potential.

- **Is it supported by the organisation?** How ready is your organisation to act? What are the barriers? Possessing the right ingredients for value creation is one thing, putting them together in the right way to make it work is another. Designing the right structure for the chosen strategy takes good leadership and communication skills.

Answer Yes to all four and you have sustainable competitive advantage!

 **tip**

Value creation potential is always asymmetrical in an industry. In other words, if everyone has access to the same things, those things are not strategically valuable.[7]

Looking for sources of advantage from what is inside an organisation is not always simple. For one thing, if you hang on to core knowledge or a core competence for too long, it can become obsolete and counter-productive for value creation. Harvard professor Dorothy Leonard-Barton calls these **core rigidities**.[8]

In the 1980s Tom Peters' and Robert Waterman's book *In Search of Excellence* became a huge bestseller and flavour of the month, but defining 'excellence' proved difficult for organisations set up with a traditional, competitive positioning format. Excellence is transitory, and not only will competitors react if they see the same source of competitive advantage available to them, the environment and context of what makes any element work in your favour is constantly shifting.

This makes feeling that you have attained progress difficult, and some companies find themselves stuck in a cycle of constant internal reinvention. If this has happened to you, or is happening to you now, you will know how very draining it can be for all concerned!

Assessing competitive advantage: conducting a resource audit

If strategy is about reacting to the future as it emerges bit by bit over time, then the strength of Porter's view is that it makes you aware of some of the components of your context. Awareness of the relationships that make up your industry does give some control – if you can translate it into sensible choices of what to do next. If strategy is about determining your own future, then success is based on unique access to scarce resources *and* the skills to manage them. Overleaf are three sources of competitive advantage proposed by the economist John Kay (architecture, reputation and innovation). In each case, you can carry out your own resource audit (because

I want this book to be applicable to anyone working in middle and operational management, let us focus on those relevant to the business unit level).[9]

Architecture

Architecture is about how clever the organisation is at managing itself and maintaining its distinctive culture. Getting this wrong is often why mergers and acquisitions run into trouble. But, get it right and you have a recipe for success, as McDonald's has shown.

brilliant tips

- **Audit financial and physical assets:** the cash flows that keep your organisation afloat and the funds for future investment (such as lines of credit or new capital); in addition, the plant, machinery and equipment, tools, land and offices needed to implement a plan. This may be measured by analysis of key financial ratios or by reflection on the financial statements of the business.

- **Audit processes and systems:** the various ways that information is used and the capacity of the practical operations employed in the organisation to deliver new as well as existing procedures and processes.

- **Audit human capital:** the people who work in the organisation and their general level of education and training, the skills and also the motivation of the employees, and the capacity of the organisation to retain, grow or find talent in the future. Cultural awareness and commitment, as well as the flexibility to learn and change, may be critical for a new strategic direction.

Reputation

Reputation can take years to establish – and moments to destroy. What people think of you is as much a source of advantage as anything else. Loyalty from customers (or suppliers) happens when you practise what you preach. Markets can spot a fake reputation, but will reward genuine trust with trust. In recent years, budget airline Ryanair has begun to work on this as a source of differentiation (mainly to gain distance from the public's image of the Ryanair of old!).

practise what you preach

brilliant tip

Audit relationships. What other people think of you can either enable or restrict how well a chosen and new strategic direction will be received. As such, and even though there is often no easy way to measure it, reputation is part of your resource audit. The wrong perception can destroy value, whilst the right location and network can help boost it.

Innovation

Innovation is the most difficult of the three to recognise as a competitive advantage. Investing in the new carries all sorts of uncertainties and risks and if an organisation believes it has been successful in the past, there will be even greater resistance to change that leads to innovation. People who are put in charge of things are generally conservative and they will want to change the fewest number of things to achieve the maximum results. Conversely, an organisation that believes its advantage lies in being the first mover may be able to embrace innovation to its fullest.

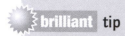

brilliant tip

Audit intellectual property and know-how, including unique or historical areas of expertise (as an organisation) or registered trademarks, patents and any inventions or innovations. What is the capacity of the organisation to attain and protect existing know-how?

In smaller organisations, and in parts or units of larger organisations, this level of initial analysis can be enough of an overview to pick out where the greatest risk to a new venture or strategy lies. A more involved analysis may require significant input from the players involved and from functional experts within the organisation.

You may also use external consultants, many of whom may have developed considerable expertise in auditing resources and analysing the results. One example of this is in the McKinsey 7-S Framework, (Figure 4.3) developed by Tom Peters and others in 1980.[10] They wanted firms to stop falling into the trap of thinking that strategic plans only need leadership to succeed. Shifting the structure of an organisation means understanding the system first. In the 7-S Framework, the soft and the hard are given equal importance.

The seven elements are:

- **Strategy:** the expression of the overall plan or direction for the organisation as it prepares to manage change. This may be explicit or implicit (or, most likely, a combination) and either widely known or obscure.
- **Structure:** the hierarchy within the organisation, the design of tasks, functions and various divisions of labour. Structure is never static. With growth comes the need to

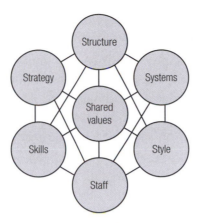

Figure 4.3 The McKinsey 7-S Framework
Source: Peters, T.J. and Waterman, R.H. (1982) 'In Search of Excellence'. McKinsey & Company.

divide, with further growth, the need to consolidate and diversify, which leads to more dividing . . . and so on. In time of strategic implementation, which parts of the structure have greater importance? How can all the parts be made to work together?

- **Skills:** the core competences, capabilities and similar type of resources possessed by the organisation (rather than by any individual in the company). This is sometimes expressed by asking what an organisation does best, which is not the same as asking how it is organised or funded. A change in strategic direction might require it to become good at something new.

- **Staff:** a measurement not of head-count, but of the sum of potential these people create as an overall resource to the organisation. The right staff should create a capability measured as a synergy.

- **Style:** the unwritten rules of how things are done, of what is acceptable or unacceptable behaviour and the tone set by the people at the top of the organisation. What is the atmosphere like and what are the norms? Does the CEO walk around talking to people or are they reclusive? Is everyone capable of playing their part?

- **Systems:** all the procedures needed to run the organisation, the processes to acquire and use information and the operations to get things done. Are these the glue that hold your organisation together or the glue that sticks the whole mechanism rigid in place, unable to move?

- **Shared values:** both the original purpose and intention of the founders when the organisation was established and the core beliefs that are the starting point of any plan for strategic implementation. What is the collective wish as expressed in the legacy people would like to leave?

 **brilliant** questions

Can you identify a recent corporate or business strategy initiative in your organisation (the bigger, the better)? Using the 7-S Framework as a guide and hindsight, did the leadership miss anything?

The 7-S Framework and the resource audit can help as simple diagnostic checklists in the preparation of strategy. Equally, they can assist in a more in-depth report and feedback to monitor the effects of the implementation of a new strategy once it is under way.

Putting it all together: political industries and dynamic capabilities

This chapter has covered quite a chunk of strategy in *industry positioning* and the *resource-based view*. Both approaches are still popular, but will have to adapt to some criticism:

● The positioning school must acknowledge that industries are not apolitical and that organisations exist in a much messier and more inter-connected world than the fans of analysis had realised. Outside-in, it turns out, did not reach very far out.

● Generic strategies look fine on paper, but that is usually where they stay (or end up). They were designed for larger corporations with Anglo-Saxon business and management cultures. The world is full of other possibilities; big is not always better and simply clustering things into similar boxes for the sake of analysis misses the point and – more worryingly – fails to explain the variety of business strategies out there.

● The resource-based view must accept that innovation needs the capacity of the organisation to be moving at a rate equal to or greater than the rate of change in the environment.[11] David Teece, an American academic who specialises in organisational development, calls these **dynamic capabilities.**

brilliant recap

Here is a summary of the main ideas that you can apply or bring to your own practice as a manager:

● Competitive advantage is a popular way of defining how strategy makes sense at the level of a business unit or profit centre.

● In stable business environments and in static market conditions, analysis can make a significant contribution to a planning process.

● Generic strategies are useful shortcuts to evaluate the basic options of differentiating yourself from your competition.

▶

> ● Auditing your internal resources can be a structured exercise designed to analyse where you currently stand.
>
> Dynamic capabilities suggest agility as quite an important factor in maintaining competitiveness. Agility moves us closer to the next way of understanding how to be a brilliant business strategist – learning and innovation.

References

[1] A cluster organisation provides a specific service in a geographical area to bring together business with similar profiles.

[2] Tovstiga, G. (2013) *Strategy in Practice: A Practitioner's Guide to Strategic Thinking*. 2nd Ed. London: John Wiley.

[3] Interestingly, though many Japanese companies did have a cost advantage, they did not have a grand strategy to compete in the USA in this way. A whole set of other factors, many to do with chance, were nearly always at play. Henry Mintzberg has more on this in his 2005 book, *Strategy Safari: Your Complete Guide Through the Wilds of Strategic Management*.

[4] http://www.benettiyachts.it/

[5] Bowman, C. and Faulkner, D. (1995) *Competitive and Corporate Strategy*. Illinois: Irwin Professional Publishing.

[6] Schilling, M.A. (2013) *Strategic Management of Technological Innovation*. New York: McGraw-Hill Education, International Ed, p. 117.

[7] You might spot here that this could make benchmarking a bit shortsighted and risky!

[8] Leonard-Barton, D. (1993) 'Core capabilities and core rigidities: A paradox in managing new product development', *Strategic Management Review* 13, 111–125.

[9] Kay, J. (1993) *Foundations of Corporate Success: How Business Strategies Add Value*. Oxford: Oxford University Press.

[10] Waterman, R., Peters, T.J. and Phillips, J. (1980) 'Structure is not organization', *Business Horizons,* June.

[11] There is a danger here, too, if the actions of the organisation are actually accelerating the rate of change in the environment: things can quickly get out of control.

CHAPTER 5

Strategy as learning and innovation

If you can dream – and not make
dreams your master;
If you can think – and not make
thoughts your aim;
If you can meet with Triumph and
Disaster
And treat those two impostors just
the same.

Rudyard Kipling (1909) *'If'*, *Rewards
and Fairies*

How this chapter will help you

Strategic planning is a formal and analytical process. Nevertheless, as boxer Mike Tyson once said, 'Everybody has a plan until they get punched in the mouth', and strategists find out that many informal and intuitive lessons are learned in the field. This chapter shows how you identify a learning organisation and demonstrates the importance of learning as you go, coming up with new ways of dealing with the world around you, using the capabilities of the organisation to innovate.

Introduction

I have no idea where in the world you are as you read these words, but I do know when – now. Your tomorrow is still to come and exists for you only in present time thought. Your past is only what you bring back to your mind, also in the now. Few people have an accurate sense of the future; we are clever only after the fact. The size of the betting industry shows that we are not very good at prediction.[1] Worryingly, because of our addiction to analysis, we are also not great at letting go of the past.[2]

> we are not great at letting go of the past

 questions

You do not let go of the past by rejecting, abandoning or denying it (denial actually holds you to the past even more firmly), but by understanding and accepting it. As a brilliant business strategist, you require more than the technical skills of analysis and planning; you also need to appreciate how an organisation learns and the different ways it can innovate.

 'The future cannot be predicted, but futures can be invented.'

Dennis Gabor[3]

When it comes to learning, many managers and organisations have their eye on the wrong things. Have you ever watched one of those television news reports about a person who has reached remarkable old age? Notice how, invariably, they are asked for the secret of a long life (admit it, you listen to their reply, don't you?), just in case they can teach us something. Unfortunately, you are not going to learn much. Studying what remains is a common thinking prejudice amongst strategists and has a name – **survivor bias.** You would be much better off studying those who did not make it! The same is true in business. For every Bill Gates and Microsoft, or Steve Jobs and Apple, there are thousands of equally clever people and companies that failed.

brilliant tip

Those who have failed either did not predict or could not adapt to change. We can sometimes learn more about success by studying failure.

Strategic decisions normally are based on analysis of what you already know. You would be forgiven for thinking that strategists must be prudent, cautious, analytical and logical. To be fair, it appears that this approach has been very successful. We are lucky, most of us, to live at a time to enjoy the fruits of the free-market economy and a second technological revolution, which are supporting an unprecedented rise in living standards for billions of people. But isn't this strategy for a solid-state universe? Is evidence from the past the best way to construct the future?

There are signs we no longer live in such a world.

In August 2015 (and note: this was via a video released on Facebook), President Obama announced plans for the Clean Power Plan, a range of federal rules aimed at getting US states, by 2030, to cut greenhouse gas emissions from their power plants by 32 per cent of 2005 levels.[4]

 'We are the first generation to feel the impacts of climate change, and the last generation to be able to do something about it.'

Barack Obama[5]

How do you continue to create value in a world where you cannot predict what will happen, and where the pace of change is accelerating? The answer we currently have is in two parts:

1 Know how to *learn*.
2 Know how to *innovate*.

Every business model has three components from which it can create value: through **legacy assets** (the assets you already own), **organic growth opportunities** or **radical change and innovation**. It may be the last of these that has the most potential to create value.

It is the end of competitive advantage!

At least, so says Columbia business professor Rita McGrath in her 2013 book of the same title.[6] She did not mean that the whole idea was dead, but rather that achieving a *sustainable* competitive advantage is no longer possible. This is because we live in a world where any advantage is transient and short-lived. Gone, she says, is the static idea of an industry, and we should instead start thinking about competing in an *arena*.

start thinking about
competing in an arena

brilliant definition

Arena

This is a dynamic place for drama and imagination; a space where you perform.

Most organisations spend all their time and energy keeping pace with the change they know about. They do not sit around slowly, carefully and analytically deliberating the next move and nor do they prepare themselves too much for the kind of change they cannot see yet.

brilliant question

The future is *always* uncertain (until it happens). What would you say is the strategist's primary job – to seek out what is known or what is unknown?

What happens is a kind of compromise between known and unknown and between planned and emergent. Henry Mintzberg shows how a company's realised strategy is always formed (not formulated) by their original, planned intentions being affected by emerging patterns over time, shown in Figure 5.1.

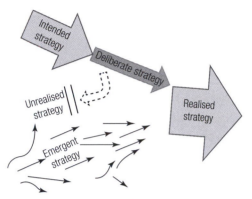

Figure 5.1 Mintzberg's emergent path to a realised strategy
Source: Mintzberg, H., Ahlstrand, B. and Lampel, J. (2008) *Strategy Safari: Your Complete Guide Through the Wilds of Strategic Management.* 2nd Ed. Harlow: FT Prentice Hall. Reproduced with permission of Pearson Education Limited, © Henry Mintzberg, Bruce Ahlstrand and Joseph Lampel 1998, 2009.

The learning organisation

Your organisation may be agile and even have excellent short-term memory, but does it have the resources it will need to adapt for the world in 20 or 30 years' time? There is a connection between strategy and learning, and between learning and change. For an organisation to deliver on its strategic objectives it must find and keep customers at a rate ahead of the rate of change in its environment.

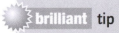 **brilliant** tip

As the business environment changes over time, so will most sources of advantage that you possess.

If everyone around you could get hold of the same resources as you (including the same calibre of people), the only strategic advantage available to you would be the capacity of your organisation to adapt and change as it goes along.

 **definition**

Learning organisation

This is an organisation that supports a culture where *everyone* is encouraged to think critically, take risks and make mistakes in order to learn from experience.

there is a strong belief in sharing and not hiding knowledge

In a learning organisation there is a strong belief in sharing and not hiding knowledge. Change, or the flexibility to change, is incorporated into day-to-day activities. The concept is an extension of the resource-based strategy and became known after the 1990 publication of *The Fifth Discipline* by Peter Senge. An MIT Professor, Senge applied some fundamental principles of human interaction to learning:

- **Personal mastery:** self-knowledge and continual practice in being aware of yourself. This is close to a current interest in **mindfulness** amongst many companies, but has also been reinforced by the recent interest in coaching.

- **Mental models:** all our assumptions, maps, filters, schemas and ways of interpreting the world, whether visible to us or not.

- **Building shared vision:** a process by which people get drawn together in commitment to a really engaging and long-term idea.

- **Team learning:** this happens when the power of a group is supported by the structure of the organisation. Team learning is personal mastery used to realise a shared vision and is a collective phenomenon created through open dialogue.

● **Systems thinking;** the fifth discipline of the title, for Senge this is the one (like Tolkien's infamous ring) to unite them all. Your company is what it is from the interaction of wholes, not parts, he says. Unfortunately, it is very hard for us to see this because we tend to focus on cut-up events, not patterns.

Senge's work was written for practising managers but if they were looking for quick fixes and templates, then this is at odds with the holistic message from systems thinking. When office politics dictate that only the results for the next quarter matter, a book with the long-term view as its message is not going to solve your issues. Personal mastery requires time and effort devoted to it. And it is a goal that is difficult to quantify.

On the other hand, can you really afford to remain ignorant of this? As a 21st century, forward-thinking strategist, you could learn something from the work of Donald Schön, an American academic who, in 1973, already had seen how an organisation (whether business, community or society) learns.[7] Long before the internet or the spread of networked global industries, he predicted that the old, hierarchical way of organising and managing was putting many companies in danger of extinction. What had delivered success so far would no longer provide the stable base for the future.

 'The world we have created today as a result of the thinking thus far has problems which cannot be solved by thinking the way we thought when we created them.'

Albert Einstein

Einstein has a point. If you always do what you have always done, the saying goes, then you will always get what you always got. The brilliant business strategist must up their game. If they do not, they will be doomed to repeat mistakes.

Knowledge

There are two ways you can show that an organisation has learned; either when a *familiar* stimulus produces a *new* response, or a *new* stimulus produces a *familiar* response. You know you are *in* a learning organisation when its whole structure can shift from the status quo and not fall to bits. The test of a learning organisation, and of any strategy, is not whether it has a grand plan from on-high but whether it has brought together strategic knowing and action at every level.

 'Knowledge workers are the people who work differently from the people of industrial and agricultural age and use their head more than their muscle.'

Peter Drucker[8]

The currency of business is no longer cash, but knowledge. Such a statement is likely to make many accountants and finance directors twitch, and it is true that you will not stick around long without enough money, but – as Drucker hinted – for over 50 years that alone has not been enough.

the currency of business is no longer cash, but knowledge

'Knowledge isn't about what you know, it's about what you don't know, and being prepared to say "I'll find out".'

Ken Robinson[9]

When you think about it, there are two kinds of knowledge at work in an organisation:

● **What people know, learn or unlearn whilst they work there:** this sort of knowledge is mobile; CEOs in FTSE 100 companies typically stay in the job for about only five years.[10] Many middle managers see three years as a reasonable time-span before moving on. Strategic issues and initiatives, however, unfold over much longer periods than a manager's tenure in position and, for this reason, you must rely on a different type of knowledge.

● **What is retained by the system:** much harder to identify and held, somehow, by the organisation itself. In businesses that do well, the connections, habits and the spreading or sharing (rather than the stockpiling or storage) of knowledge lies at the heart of productivity and competitiveness.

Knowledge is weird stuff. For a start, a lot of what you know you cannot easily express. Its value depends entirely on context; knowing how to build and sail a boat is not much use in the middle of a desert, whilst if you *were* on a desert island, knowing what Porter's Five Forces are would not be terribly valuable.

 **definition**

Knowledge

Swedish businessman Karl-Erik Sveiby, often referred to as the father of knowledge management, defines knowledge as the combination of:

● **know-what:** the facts, opinions and beliefs that are the raw material for deciding what to do;

● **know-how:** our capacity to act and the skills we get from practice, procedures, and rules.[11]

It took about 45 years for the telephone to reach 50 per cent market penetration in the United States, but the smartphone needed around only seven years to do the same.[12] Know-what is useless if no one is looking after the flow of know-how. Plus, you need a third – *know-why*.

brilliant questions

What type of knowledge do you think is crucial to your business? Do you spend resources on trying to capture it or on trying to move it along? Do you think knowledge is power? Why?

As you ponder these questions, I want to share eight practical ways you can help your organisation become more like a learning organisation.

1. Be a role model

The higher you are in your organisation, the more visible as a role model you become to others. But in a learning organisation,

being a good role model is important at *every* level. The factory shop
floor employee who 'walks the talk'
of experimenting to make things better can be as powerful an example to

**be passionate in, and
about, what you do**

others as the CEO. Be passionate in, and about, what you do.
Above all, be curious. Curiosity is at the heart of learning and
leads to experimentation and discovery.

 **tip**

'Tell us what you know' – a brilliant business strategist will actively
encourage others to share knowledge and information, by all means
possible. They will start by sharing what they know.

2. Tell stories

Organisations are informal networks every bit as much as they
are formal ones. Knowledge and lessons from learning circu-
late best when people know what has contributed to success.
For the business strategist, narrative is very important. Find
examples where objectives have been met.

3. Find a way (if you can) to measure the firm's human capital[13]

Some managers like to examine how much they spend on training, glancing at what the participant evaluations were, before
asking whether or not there was an outcome on the bottom
line. This is not a very good way.

4. Celebrate success and reward risk-taking

There are many award schemes that will help you record and
recognise commitment to learning. Some, such as the ISO
certification processes, are well known, others are local or

industry-specific, but they can rally efforts. Make employees responsible and accountable and make their learning something for which they are rewarded. *Every* deviation from plan is an opportunity to learn and every tension you meet is a potential source of creativity.

5. Learn from your employees

The people closest to how the organisation functions have valuable knowledge. Tap into it. Many of Japan's top companies owe their success to a shared commitment between management and workers to remain employed by that organisation for their entire career. Management may be centralised and status-driven in Asian corporations, but decisions are arrived at through group discussion and consensus. Although time-consuming, this means that strategy can be implemented quickly because everyone already understands it. By contrast, it has become almost impossible for knowledge-based businesses in Western economies to work this way.

 'Always treat your employees exactly as you want them to treat your best customers.'

Stephen R. Covey

6. Learn from your customers (when things go wrong)

Your customers can be your best source of information and it is important that you have a dialogue with them. But, as you will see in this chapter, if you devote all your energy to keeping only your best customers happy, you can become very vulnerable to strategic drift.

7. Learn from your competition

Actually, this is a no-brainer. The real question is, who is your competition? How you answer this will define most of the boundaries to thinking within your own organisation.

8. Protect your organisation's intellectual property (IP) only if <u>not</u> doing so would destroy value

IP can include trademarks and brands, copyrights and patents, but also it can be how you handle confidential information, market research insights, or the way that you educate and train people within the organisation. It is easy to become overly obsessive about this, though. Some of the best learning organisations use open sharing as their strategy for finding new and better ways of doing business.

This all sounds great, doesn't it? Do not forget that strategic problems are never easy to solve, and all of the above require leadership and followership to create the right conditions for dialogue and trust (essential components of the learning organisation). And a lot can get in the way of learning in organisations. Here are four typical barriers:

Information overload

Learning needs time, and space, for reflection. If your day is a series of emails, meetings and constant catching-up on deadlines and targets, it is likely that you will be drowning in the details rather than seeing the bigger picture. I see it very often amongst Executive MBAs – the better they are doing at their jobs, the more work gets piled on top of them and there is so much noise that they are unable to separate the important from the trivial.

The imposter syndrome

A surprising number of people, managers included, are unsure about how they have got where they are. Most people do not plan to end up in executive roles: they are given more responsibility as they go. Eventually they feel out of their depth, in positions they are not convinced they are qualified for. Secretly they worry that someone is going to expose them as a fraud and this can make them cautious about sharing knowledge or admitting they do not have all the answers. Neither of these attributes are what a strategist needs.

'Not invented here'

New ideas and new ways of doing things can be threatening. People feel very protective of their own turf. 'Better the devil you know' is often the kind of sentiment. This is a barrier to accepting change to the status quo imposed from outside. It is also symptomatic of a 'them & us' culture, which itself is always a symptom of a deeper strategic issue.

'It's easy to come up with new ideas; the hard part is letting go of what worked for you two years ago, but will soon be out of date.'

Roger von Oech

A blame culture

You would think a blame culture would be easy to spot, but they are often silent and invisible as people learn not to put their heads above the parapet. When no one openly takes any unnecessary risks, reports errors, or admits any mistakes, you know you are in a blame culture. Mistakes will be happening, under the surface, but with no one learning from them. It may be tempting to point the finger at the leadership, but remember that the problem may be systemic.

Depressing stuff, right? The good news is that there are many great examples of organisations that are exploring a much more positive future. The strongest indication of this is when you see evidence of **innovation,** which appears in a learning organisation as fruit does on a tree. Innovation is the second route to value creation.

The rise of innovation

Humans are an inherently inventive species and organisations either get in the way of this fact or they embrace it. Sadly, many managers are completely unaware or, worse, do not believe that this is so.

Creativity can be chaotic and unpredictable. It is anarchic, fun and very hard to plan or control. Part of the charm of being truly creative is that you have no idea at the start whether what you come up with at the end will be any use, or of any value to your business. What organisations need is not necessarily creativity, but innovation.

 **definition**

Innovation

Innovation follows invention and is a special category of creativity. Every innovation is a creative act, but not every creative act is an innovation. *In strategy, only those things that contribute to the creation of value are innovations.*

Innovation is targeted. It may be targeted to meet a specific problem or goal and then channelled through strategy.

Disruptive innovation

A special class of innovation was coined by Clayton Christensen, a Harvard Business School professor. He identified two types:

- **High-level refinement:** the action of an organisation seeking to maintain a traditional definition of competitive advantage. To stay ahead of its rivals, a company will work hard to introduce new and additional features that a customer might see as a benefit worth paying more for. Christensen calls this sort of tweaking *sustaining innovations*. Successful companies will always offer their best customers what they ask for. You can't really beat an established company at their own game because they will always be more profitable than you at the top end.

- **Low-level disruption:** the introduction of a more simple and often much cheaper alternative technology, product or service. Because market leaders target high-profit customers, they leave the door open at the bottom end. This usually goes unnoticed at first because existing players are so focused on high-level refinements. But new entrants can become game-changers and even threaten to put the big, established players out of business through *disruptive innovations*.

The classic example of disruptive innovation, according to Christensen, was the introduction of the desk-top PC, not seen as a real threat by the big mainframe computer companies, who were listening only to existing customers. Eventually, of course, the PC brought the computing power of a mainframe first to every office desk and then to every home. Now the smartphone and tablet computer raise similar questions for the PC success stories. Will they remain viable? They may start out low-level, but disruptive innovations can end up being seismic shifts that change the whole landscape for everyone doing business.

 **example**

The sharing economy

In the space of just a few years, the world has embraced the use of the internet and mobile technology. The economic potential of the World Wide Web was realised early on by a number of companies, and not only the obvious candidates supplying goods and services to consumers, such as Apple, Amazon and PayPal. Many bricks and mortar businesses, including Wal-Mart and Staples, have extended their activities online to exploit the internet's potential for segmentation and speed of access.

Alongside this economic boom in consumption, consumer-to-consumer Web portals such as eBay, Alibaba and TripAdvisor introduced new business models that exploited a Web 2.0 (user-generated) inspired sort of consumerism. Here, end users become suppliers and the currency of trust is in the form of positive buyer/user feedback. At the beginning, these sites complemented rather than threatened the big online retailers, who focused on high-end additions (e.g. Amazon Prime).

A door to disruption may have appeared in a more recent and dramatic shift in consumer behaviour, part of a grass-roots movement known as the **collaborative** (or **sharing**) **economy.** We are being steered from the outright ownership of goods to their temporary sharing or renting, and from the one-to-many transactions of large organisations to one-to-one transactions between individuals. Social media can reach and activate people and is the most obvious sign that the collaborative economy is scalable. In the 2008 US Presidential campaign, for example, Barack Obama's team used innovative messaging via Facebook, email, text and phone to connect with traditionally under-empowered voters. Collaboration was a core element of the success of the strategy, as was real-time feedback on which tactics were resonating.

The collaborative economy represents an alternative to modern consumerism. New online businesses are working with lower margins, targeting smaller markets with much simpler products and services, with ▶

what the big, established giants would not see as attractive solutions – the classic signs of disruptive innovation. Many players in the collaborative economy exist also with a mission to create communities that educate consumers, where there is an eye on social capital, not just economic value. For others, though the sharing of a positive experience is good, the goal is also monetary and the desire to grow is paramount. A prominent example is the accommodation site Airbnb. Founded in 2008, by 2013 it was supplying 6 million nights of accommodation, despite not owning a single room and by 2015 it had a market valuation of $20 billion. Another case is transportation network company Uber, which is rapidly expanding its crowd-sourced business model of independent drivers to major cities around the world. It expects revenues of $10 billion in 2015.

Disruptive innovation starts by providing simpler, more direct and cheaper alternatives to the over-engineered and over-sophisticated mainstream. Regulators are currently struggling to keep up with disruptive changes and many traditional businesses are lobbying to protect their assets.

Airbnb and Uber grab headlines, but industry insiders see these as the tip of an iceberg of possible connections in a sharing economy that includes holiday properties, rental of designer clothing, pooled car journeys and barter, as well as crowdfunding for new start-ups. The real challenge for mainstream businesses will be how to respond. The UK's largest clothing retailer, Marks and Spencer, for example, launched a scheme for recycling clothes to charity called *shwopping*, and in 2013 global car renter Avis purchased car-share company Zip Car. It remains to be seen whether others, such as the major hotel chains, will have to abandon or change their basic business models.

Why are so many well-established and profitably managed organisations susceptible to disruptive innovation? Inertia will keep an organisation in place and unconventional research and development may be unpopular if it cannot show immediate payback. Implementing innovation may require re-skilling or investment in new equipment. Innovation can also undermine the confidence staff have in the organisation. If you detect potential disruption to your business or industry, you need to bear in mind three things:

1 **Leadership:** convincing others that things really are going to change and then getting them to move with you. At the same time as bringing others with you on a journey of learning and change, you will need to be rigorous in weighing up the risks involved.

2 **Partnership:** being prepared to reach out to new and surprising partners who have untapped areas of knowledge. These might be in your value chain (upstream as in distributors and customers, or downstream as in suppliers), indirect competitors, technology developers, or totally unrelated businesses that have developed successful business models (benchmarking). Partnerships can help you find temporary niches for your innovation until it can be scaled up.

3 **Stewardship:** the responsible planning, care of and use of resources. It is an iterative, developmental process involving the creation of shared understandings with the aim of choosing service over self-interest. A strategist should always take this seriously and remain actively interested in the views of others, as this brings awareness to themselves.

Innovation can appear in every sphere of business, as this example shows.

> innovation can appear in every sphere of business

 **example**

Glasto!

The Glastonbury Festival of Contemporary Performing Arts in Somerset is one of the best-known and largest outdoor events in the world. From a small and intermittent music festival in the early 1970s, it has grown and adapted to changes in society and music taste and now easily attracts attendances ▶

of over 175,000 each June. Glastonbury retains some of the alternative free spirit and creative ethos of its founders, chief of whom is the festival landowner, Michael Eavis. Eavis has retained a commitment to support charitable causes and social enterprises, but balances this with economic reality. Commercial enterprises operate on site, festival headline acts are often chosen to capitalise on public interest, and the site is protected from illegal entry of non-ticket holders by a 'superfence' patrolled by security teams.

Glastonbury used not to make money, but innovation has sustained this event as the world around it has changed. Examples of innovation at Glastonbury over the years have included wind-generated power for and televised coverage of the main stage (these days broadcast means live-streaming of all stages), the expansion of entertainment areas and zones to encompass every style of music and art, a silent disco, biodegradable tent pegs handed out free to all campers, free entry for under 13s, and complete festival access and a dedicated campsite for the disabled.

Glastonbury's reputation is such that tickets usually sell out in hours, even before the line-up of featured artists has been announced. The challenge for the organisers, now headed by Eavis' daughter Emily, may be maintaining the freshness and excitement for this top live event in the future. There are now in excess of 100 other outdoor festivals in the UK alone, so festival regulars have choice. Will Glastonbury become vulnerable to disruptive innovation?

Innovation as a source of competitive advantage

Innovation is not restricted to new goods or services from the research and development arm of your business. Innovative advantage can come from many different directions, such as:

- changes in the operations of distribution or production;
- the creative use of media channels to reach new or existing markets;
- original sources of finance and investment.

Innovation is always contextual. It is anything you *could* do that everyone else is currently not doing. What others are doing might be novel for you, but it would not be innovation. The trouble is, the list of what everyone else is *not* doing is vast. How can you know which potential innovation is going to generate future value and be a source of advantage for you for long enough to be worth the effort? Many businesses will not risk doing something that no one else is doing, and innovation frequently results in watered-down versions of what the organisation already does – with all the pressure of payback.

Here are six tips for managing strategic innovation:

1   **Remember, ideas already exist in your organisation.** They exist in the people you work with. They know their business inside out and often see where it can be improved or reinvented, *if* you have the right culture to bring these ideas out. You will not pick up on these as a strategist if you are not in listening mode. Walk around, talk to people, ask them genuine questions.

2   **Good ideas do not have to be earth-shatteringly huge to be worth investing in.** Not every innovation is going to be, or has to be, the new smartphone, bagless vacuum cleaner or World Wide Web. More modest goals are more realistic. And anyway, many ideas that turn out to be game-changing start as modest proposals or unforeseen opportunities.

3   **Ideas spark ideas, but need space to do so.** Innovation needs to have *more* freedom in which to grow than established projects and processes, so suspend the normal controls and judgements. Give people tacit permission to talk to each other and to change their minds. Do not expect things to be decided or fixed too quickly. Your role is to stimulate invention and then have the resources to invest in those ideas that will add value to the organisation or business.

4   **Prepare to have a lot go wrong, and fail.** So what? Apple still gets lots wrong in order to get a few things right. In a learning organisation, news of failure recycles as knowledge for use in further invention.

5   **Prepare to have a lot go right, and still fail.** This is about not being fooled into a false sense of security either by your triumphs or your disasters.

6   **Innovation is a collaborative balance between the freedom to think with others and responsibility for the viability of the organisation.** Too little innovation and you will stagnate, too much and you will lose focus. Innovation for a brilliant business strategist means being completely reliant on the relationships of trust you build with those around you.

Let us pause for a moment

Whether your aim is to diversify, build a new core competence or reposition in a new, unique competing space, learning, knowledge and innovation are integral to strategy.

In short, they are key ingredients for managing strategic change. When innovation is your mindset rather than your goal, you will start coming up with new ideas. It is obvious that there is a link here between development as a strategist and development of yourself as a person. If leadership of a strategic change process leaves you unchanged as a person, you really have missed the point.

> learning, knowledge and innovation are integral to strategy

 'All types of knowledge, ultimately, mean self-knowledge.'

Bruce Lee[14]

Lee, a student of philosophy as well as martial arts, was making an observation about the tension between natural instinct and control. Relying exclusively on instinct would be unscientific. Being concerned only with order and control would make you a machine.

I rather like the way that this comes across in a dialogue between psychiatrist Dr Robin Skynner and comedian, author and *Monty Python* member John Cleese, in their 1996 book *Life And How To Survive It*. In their conversation, they highlight the relationship between order and chaos, or 'closed' and 'open' modes of thinking in the creative process. The open mode or mindset is when we are receptive to input from the world around us. We are explorers and any information or insight found helps us redraw our internal maps so that they are more detailed and accurate. This process can bring with it a sense of fun as well as adventure and is often playful and full of wit. But, as Robin Skynner points out, when we want to get something done – when action to achieve a goal is what matters – we need to switch to the 'closed' mode, which is more purposeful, single-minded and serious. As John Cleese points out, 'if you're attacking a machine-gun nest, you shouldn't make a particular effort to enjoy the scenery.' We have to be able to switch between these modes of thinking, but getting from 'open' to 'closed' is much easier than going the other way round because the closed mode stops us from being reflective, which would take us to the open way of thinking.[15]

What do you think? Is he right? And, if he is, do you identify more with the open or closed mode of thinking in your own practice?

Putting it together: disruptive trends in your own industry

As they say in Vegas, 'the house always wins', and any prediction is a gamble. Some of the disruptive trends we were all talking about some years ago do not seem to have had much impact. We are still waiting for the paperless office and the virtual organisation, for instance. The same technology fuelling those speculations has had profound effects – but few that we saw coming.

What are the trends now that point the way to the next disruptive innovation? Will we, for example, have to redraw our business models as a result of any of these?

● The use of crowdsourcing for ideas or crowdfunding for finance.

● Peer-to-peer lending and microcredit schemes in emerging economies.

● Web 3.0, and the internet of things.

● As Subway is now the world's largest restaurant chain via a franchise business model, will this open the door for newcomers in other areas.

● Carbon footprinting and carbon trading.

You can add to this list and it is fun to do so. One creative way to spot where you need to learn or innovate is to ask yourself the following (perverse) question:

brilliant (but warped) question

What is the one thing you would do to destroy your business or organisation in the shortest possible time?

brilliant recap

Here is a summary of the main ideas that you can apply or bring to your own practice as a manager:

● We are all learning, all the time. Learning and change are intertwined. Learning involves loss of 'prior ways of seeing reality – the loss of fundamental assumptions which until now had brought certainty and security'.[16] This can be tough.

- A learning organisation is one that shapes itself ready to respond to changes in its environment. Strategy emerges from what happens to your plan when it meets reality.

- The management of many kinds of knowledge is crucial. Know-how, know-what and know-why form the basis for competitive advantage in volatile new industries.

- Learning enables innovation.

- The true test of strategic innovation is whether it creates value for the organisation at a rate of return better than any alternative use of that working capital.

The groundwork for an understanding of strategy is in place. Nothing is clear-cut, but it is time now to move towards action and see how strategy affects everyday working in management.

References

[1] In the UK alone, estimated to be worth £9 billion in 2014, taken from 'Gambling and Betting Activities in the UK: Market Research Report', IBISWorld. Available from: http://www.ibisworld.co.uk/market-research/gambling-betting-activities.html

[2] Later in the book, I will return to the obvious conclusion from this – that we are not even very good at living in the present.

[3] Gabor, D. (1963) *Inventing the Future*. New York: Alfred A. Knopf, p. 207.

[4] Sources: 'Taking action on climate change: The Clean Power Plan', United States Environmental Protection Agency. Available from: http://www2.epa.gov/cleanpowerplan and BBC News (2015) 'Climate change: Obama Reveals Clean Power Plan'. 3 August. [Online]. Available from: http://www.bbc.co.uk/news/world-us-canada-33753067 [accessed: 3 August 2015].

[5] BBC News (2015) 'Climate change: Obama Reveals Clean Power Plan' [Online] 3 August 2015. Available from: http://www.bbc.co.uk/news/world-us-canada-33753067 [accessed: 13 August 2015].

[6] McGrath, R. (2013) *The End of Competitive Advantage: How to Keep Your Strategy Moving as Fast as Your Business.* Boston: Harvard Business Review Press.

[7] Schön, D.A. (1973) *Beyond the Stable State: Public and Private Learning in a Changing Society.* Harmondsworth: Penguin.

[8] Drucker, P. (1959) *Landmarks of Tomorrow.* New York: Harper & Row.

[9] Ken Robinson, 'Life is your talents discovered', TEDxLiverpool. Available from: https://www.youtube.com/watch?v=FLbXrNGVXfE

[10] Howard, S. (2014) 'CEOs: the challenge of creating a lasting legacy of sustainability', *Guardian.* 2 October. Available from: http://www.theguardian.com/sustainable-business/2014/oct/02/ceos-challenge-creating-lasting-legacy-sustainability-short-term

[11] McKenzie, J. and Van Winkelen, C. (2004) *Understanding the Knowledgeable Organization: Nurturing Knowledge Competence.* London: Cengage Learning EMEA, p. 5.

[12] DeGusta, M. (2002) 'Are Smart Phones Spreading Faster than Any Technology in Human History?' *MIT Technology Review.* 9 May. Available from: http://www.technologyreview.com/news/427787/are-smart-phones-spreading-faster-than-any-technology-in-human-history/

[13] I dare you to go and find out why . . . and, if you can, let me know. We could make a fortune!

[14] 'Bruce Lee, The Lost Interview', *The Pierre Berton Show,* Screen Gems Canada, 9 December 1971.

[15] Skynner, R. and Cleese, J. (1996) *Life And How To Survive It.* New Delhi: Cedar Books.

[16] Kim D. (1993) 'The link between individual and organizational learning', *Sloan Management Review* 35, pp. 37–50.

CHAPTER 6

Strategy, day to day

Life is just one damn thing after another.

Elbert Hubbard[1]

How this chapter will help you

Once upon a time, only three groups of people were concerned with strategy: business school academics, senior management and management consultants. To this we may now add a fourth – you. Middle managers, supervisors, technical experts, specialists and functional leaders are responsible for the resources and operations that every business relies on and this chapter will show how your day-to-day work also has a strategic side to it.

Introduction

When you are in the thick of it solving tactical problems, the externally focused world of the corporate strategist can look very remote. In fact, with work emails and texts following you home on your mobile devices, you may not get any time at all to step back and see the larger canvas. Ironically, though, the busier you get, the more you need that sense of perspective. How else will you know what to align your work to?

 **question**

How does *your* job contribute to the strategy of your organisation?

Take a moment to think about how your organisation is set up. Unless it is a start-up with everyone mucking in, chances are that what you see is the fairly well-defined division of responsibility and expertise into sections, siloes and departments. People are employed to perform specific tasks that are grouped around functions. The functions are needed to run the business. There may be many types of organisation structure, but they all seem to revolve around a limited set of internal resources. In this chapter, I am going to look at four such management resources. These all have a strategic side:

- operations management;
- management accounting and finance;
- human resources;
- marketing (this function is slightly different from the first three).

Once you see how every part of an organisation is vital to the planning and implementation of strategy, it is logical to become curious about those bits of the business with which you are less familiar.

Let us start at the top, though. CEOs are not always aware of what happens below them, as the case below highlights.

 **example**

The Undercover Boss

This is a popular TV show broadcast by Channel 4 in the UK, in which the CEO of a large chain of businesses is placed in disguise as a new/rookie member of staff and, under some pretext, is rotated around a series of roles working in key areas of their own business – but always at low levels. They get to see the results of their strategic vision through the eyes of their own employees, warts and all. Invariably this is an eye-opening and emotional experience. To their amazement, the CEO discovers that their employees are dedicated and frequently full of ideas. To their shock and dismay, they find they are also stressed and under-appreciated. During the show, staff take their (disguised) new colleague, who generally shows no aptitude for the tasks at hand, at face value. It is only at the end, and back at headquarters, where the truth is revealed. Interestingly, the CEO usually has taken time to reflect first.

What are *actually* revealed are hard-hitting lessons for the CEO, who can now act on the issues he or she has seen and feed back to the strategic initiatives the operational information and realities.[2]

At some point, even the most mechanistic CEO must come to terms with the fact that she cannot do much without the cooperation and contribution of every support function (and the people in them). Finance, accounting, human resources, marketing, operations, and a host of other activities, are what keep a company running. As orchestra conductor Benjamin Zander related in a famous TED talk:

 'I was 45 years old, I'd been conducting for 20 years, and I suddenly had a realisation. The conductor of an orchestra doesn't make a sound ... He depends, for his power, on his ability to make other people powerful. And that changed everything for me. It was totally life-changing.'

Ben Zander[3]

Operations management

In the original *Star Trek* television series and films, the ship's trustworthy chief engineer, Mr Scott (Scotty), was the archetypal operations and processes manager. Ever at the ready to deliver the forward momentum needed for his captain to achieve the mission, he is exasperated by Kirk's poor grasp of the limitations of the Enterprise's engines. Scotty's view was **the process view.**

The process view says that the effective and efficient management of an organisation's operations and systems is what *actually* generates value. Pretty much everything you do at work is part of an operation, process or system, including stock levels, production inputs and throughputs, quality, agility, capacity to meet demand, budgeting, training . . . and so on. The job of the manager is to break operations down to constituent parts (or build them up from these) in order to deliver whatever product or service the firm needs, now and into the future.

 **definition**

Operations management

The goal of operations management is to maximise the perception of value added in any and all processes that transform an organisation's inputs into its outputs.

Operations managers are experts in **business-as-usual.** When it comes to implementing strategy, however, their concern must switch to *future* requirements to transform inputs to outputs. The good news is that setting up and running operations and processes naturally involves planning, implementation and evaluation – which are exactly the same qualities used in making strategy. The bad news is that strategy often asks us to think about *not* doing business-as-usual. Direction taken towards something new and different may mean abandoning some strongly held practices and beliefs. No one knows better than the manager holding an operation or process how it throws a spanner in the works when new working practices are imposed from above.

Operations strategy

brilliant definition

Operations strategy

This describes the way that an organisation plans and prepares to meet future market needs.

Operations strategy shifts the focus from the present to the future, and from the short-term to the long-term. The operations function can be part of strategic thinking in two ways:

1 **Strategy influences (changes) the operations function:** if they are a large enough part of your business, your processes and systems may deserve a whole strategy of their own. This is a top-down approach, and you are fortunate if as a middle manager you are involved. However, you may also be in danger of losing your job if you and your department do not align to the priorities, targets and objectives set by the centre.

2 **The operations function influences (changes) strategy:** by contributing to strategic issue identification, implementation and evaluation (feedback). This is a bottom-up approach in which middle management is essential. A good CEO will always ask for a variety of opinions before acting, as they know that the organisation will get nowhere if it does not involve those doing the work in the strategic planning process.

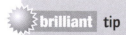

brilliant tip

The process view needs to have a voice at the top or board level.

The operations management mindset tends to be one of getting things done, solving problems, smooth running and not rocking the boat. There is nothing that hard-core operations people like more than getting their hands dirty (literally, if possible) in a good bit of analysis. The tendency to want to solve a problem, though, means that operations managers may not point out what senior management or consultants need to be aware of. Perhaps it is because when things are not functioning properly, they can be seen as yet another operational challenge to fix. The politics of the organisation can stop the flow of bad news upwards. If operations staff are not telling and CEOs are not asking, then key information on how a strategy might work or fail is not in the system.

So what sorts of contributions can be described as strategic? What has this function got to offer? Here are three ways:

1 An inside view of the **supply chain** and advice or transferable skills from the management of processes and systems. An expert in the use of the supply chain operations reference (SCOR), for example, will have valuable know-how in every step of value delivery, from sourcing to dealing with returns. This know-how can appraise plans for new systems.

2 **Quality conformance,** or how well a system or operation meets a specific standard: 'You get what you tolerate' is a management (and parenting!) truism and is why so many organisations put this at the top of their wish list when devising a new strategy. Quality is defined differently in every context, but is always an essential ingredient in strategic intent. This is clearly demonstrated in the elimination of waste in **lean manufacturing,** where operations and strategy are mutually reliant.

3 **Expertise and information** for strategists on achieving future economies of scale, flow (the time taken to perform

a process with no delays) and capacity (the amount that can be done or produced using the resources available).

A brilliant business strategist should avoid interfering with the day-to-day work of operations managers. As a strategist, tinkering with the day-to-day makes you ineffective and can be symptomatic of a lack of strategic initiatives. You should be available, not remote. Keeping in touch with how your operations staff and management experience their jobs is essential.

keeping in touch is essential

ϟbrilliant tip

Good strategists are good listeners. Although they may know their own mind and have a strong sense of vision, they are also flexible. When the facts change, the strategist changes strategy.

Like everything else in an organisation, the operations function must be focused on meeting the needs of the customer. Operations strategy can, therefore, be driven by fresh market insights. At the same time, delivery of an operation will be limited by the resources available inside the firm to carry it out. This is the evergreen external/internal split, but it has a big bearing on operations strategy because the tension between the two is not often acknowledged.

Strategic accounting and finance

 'The future is purchased by the present.'

Samuel Johnson

Money is our way of storing and quantifying the notion of value. A few companies may see it as an end in itself, but the vast majority of organisations recognise money as a means to growth, survival or service. Preserving is usually the first consideration. Most businesses could survive a month or two without a CEO (some might actually thrive!), but an operation that runs out of cash stops being a going concern and faces ruin or requires intervention.

Finance and accounting have the knack of making a lot of managers nervous. For one thing, it has its own language, which is heavy on jargon. That vocabulary is outside your control and standardised to broadly accepted micro- and macroeconomic theories. Getting finance wrong can have immediate and very visible consequences, which doesn't help calm the nerves.

Do not worry. The fact is you do not have to be an accounting expert or an investment guru to make a strategic impact – you just need to understand what those experts are trying to tell you. We have already seen how every manager is an operations manager, so it is not a huge jump to appreciate that every operational decision has a financial consequence or constraint.

> getting finance wrong can have immediate consequences

Let us look at three areas:

- management accounting;
- financial accounting;
- corporate finance.

Management accounting

Management accounting is the internal use of historical accounting information for decision making. It uses economic theory about individual actions. Nearly every manager comes across this most often in the budgets and the budgeting process (cost accounting). *Budgeting* is a process. It can be political and idiosyncratic and tends to be done differently in different companies. A *budget*, on the other hand, is an approved plan and a control mechanism and is a more standardised process. A budget extends into the future and measuring the benefit of a future managerial decision is delicate, even when there are no changes being made to how and what the organisation is trying to do. Resources are always scarce and every day you are making decisions about the best way to use what you have.

brilliant tip

Every management decision questions the best use of a given resource to create value. By consciously aligning with the overall goals and strategy of the organisation, you can move from being a reactive to a proactive manager.

Financial accounting

Financial accounting collects data from past performance to inform the leadership (and externals with an interest in how you are performing) on the current state of the business. It is a picture of the value created by all the decisions over the last year. All limited liability companies must produce a set of accounts. There are four key questions to which management needs answers:

1 What is our cash position? Do we have enough money available to pay our bills and stay in business?

2 How are we performing compared to our competitors?

3 Are we wealthier or worse off than in the past?

4 What is our financial position going to be at a given point in the future?

You can probably see how some of these will inform strategic thinking, at least in terms of stating the current position. The way that financial accounting extracts information about performance is through financial statements and the ratios they contain:

Cash-flow statement: even profitable (on paper) companies must make sure they have access to cash. The cash-flow statement puts together incoming and outgoing money from operations, investments and finance. Generating revenue allows you to generate growth without needing to borrow. A cash-flow forecast reveals levels of liquidity, which may impact on strategic implementation.

Profit and loss statement (or income statement): a record of profit (not cash) achieved in the time between two balance sheets. There are several types of profit. Gross profit is the balance between revenue and direct cost of sales. Net profit deducts from this all other expenses (such as overheads, wages, dividends and taxes) and is the famous bottom line. Because this is a measure comparable with your competitors, it is a key tool in evaluating a strategy.

Balance sheet: a snapshot of what economic assets the firm owns versus what are its obligations to others (hence the balance) on a given day, compared to what it owned and owed on the same day a year earlier. The basic formula is *total assets = total liabilities.*

Financial ratios: shortcuts – sources of information that a financial analyst might bring to the strategy process and that middle and senior managers might refer to in making judgement on value. So, it is worth you knowing what the main ones indicate, but not how to calculate them.

The forms of accounting summarised above are the bread and butter of management decision making in the world of business-as-usual. It is when a strategic decision or plan requires the use of funds that the organisation does not actually have that finance itself becomes strategic. Notice, as with operations, a future orientation changes everything. Major decisions can involve the need to seek sources of investment for capital expenditure as well as growth strategies (such as acquisition or international expansion). Whoever is doing that funding will need reassurance that they are going to get a return. Therefore, your job is to know what that return will be.

> a future orientation changes everything

Corporate finance

A key question for a brilliant business strategist is where to put resources to produce better return on investment than the cost of capital. Corporate finance is the assessment and measure of future value. Decisions here involve:

- what actions produce free cash flows;
- where to source funds;
- whether surpluses should be distributed as dividend or reinvested.

Valuation is *the* central concept of corporate finance. Knowing what your business is worth is where you begin in your series of judgements and decisions about growing, diversifying or refocusing the business. There will certainly be other considerations than money, of course, but the maximisation of value and minimisation of risk are rarely far from a CEO's thoughts. Most proposed strategies are judged on their promise to produce an economic return – usually a *discounted cash flow* (DCF) that exceeds a hurdle rate – often the *opportunity cost of capital* (OCC). If your strategy is based on competitive advantage, for instance, you will select a hypothetical time horizon by when you think your competitors will have caught up with you. The resulting **competitive advantage period** (CAP) is when you may say that the economic return is generating value. After that you would need a further round of planning to find a new source of advantage.

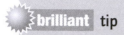 **tip**

A business is worth what it can be expected to do in the future, not the past.

Corporate finance is a tool for two things:

1 **Quantifying the effects of strategy:** be careful, though. Predicting what is going to happen during your planning period is not exactly a science. You can manage risk but not eliminate it, so what counts for acceptable in risk and return varies a lot, depending on many other variables. Corporate finance is a very human activity despite its apparent love for numbers.

2 **Informing strategic change to capital structure:** capital structure is the equity and the debt inside the firm, and every company needs to find the right balance between the two. Altering this through a change in strategy can happen through:

- mergers, acquisitions and strategic alliances;
- a **leveraged buyout** by institutional investors;
- **spinning off** a profitable part of your business as a separate entity;
- **divestment** (in the private sector) **or privatisation** (in the public sector) of an unwanted or non-core asset;
- bankruptcy.

For all its importance, money does not make the world go round – people do. Granted, people who think only about money will think that it is the money talking, but it is human beings – the next strategic resource – that decide strategy. When you seek strategic direction in managerial decision making, consider the following steps:

- Define, clearly, the issue.
- Create a broad list of alternative courses of action.
- Narrow down the list to those that are *viable* and within scope of the strategy.
- Calculate the financial cost-benefit for each.

brilliant tip

The most common way of doing this is by discounting future cash flows to find the **net present value** (NPV) of a future action. If the present value of future value (e.g. income) exceeds the present value of what the future costs, then that course of action can be said to add value to the organisation.

- Include those non-financial factors that have a bearing on the decision or choice.
- Come to a decision.

Strategic human resource management (SHRM)

'What's the use of happiness? It can't buy you money.'

Henny Youngman

'People' ought to be an easy subject for any manager to master. After all, managers are people, too. But it seems by the time they are placed into a management level where this is important, most managers feel a bit helpless. Money they can figure out. Processes they can control. But people? Managing the work of others involves three sets of choices with strategic impact:

1 **Task:** what work will need to be done in the future?

2 **Talent:** what sorts of people with what sorts of skills, education and training?

3 **Purpose:** why will it need to be done? Who will benefit and how?

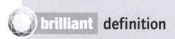
lead, yes, but command, no

People are a resource that no strategist should ignore. There is no value in manipulating people *en masse*. Lead, yes, but command, no. On the other hand, every organisation relies on the talent at its disposal to achieve the objectives it sets itself. Human resource management is as old as employment but has become a major function in organisational design only over the last 50 years or so. *Strategic* HRM is even newer than that.

brilliant definition

Strategic HRM

This has been defined as 'a distinctive approach to employment management which seeks to achieve competitive advantage through the strategic development of a highly committed and capable workforce, using an array of cultural, structural and personnel techniques.'[4]

As you see from this definition, many HR strategy consultants believe that HRM is a component of competitive advantage.

This is not easy to prove and if they mean the knowledge that people carry around with them, then notoriously this can fairly easily walk out of the building. A more insightful way of looking at this would be to say that a *human-capital advantage* (this is the phrase used) occurs when:

● an organisation's HR processes and systems, organisational culture (with the shared language, trust and values, salary benefits, network of relationships this entails) are all consistently superior to its competitors . . .

meaning that . . .

● it can attract and retain more talented employees for longer than its rivals, because they think it is a better place to work.

What matters, strategically, is not hiring clever people per se but building excellent systems of recruitment, training, retention, reward and motivation for the future. These operations and processes are your true competitive advantage because they help you attract the people your competitors would love to have.

brilliant tip

If you are the boss, find out what your employees think of your organisation's HR strategy (have you ever asked them?). First, you might want to ask them to tell you what they think that strategy is – that could be more revealing.

This is forgotten at the board level, where SHRM rarely has an equal seat. They may delegate to a lower management level, but down there everyone is already overloaded with other things to do. To make matters worse, when the going gets tough, and belts need tightening, training and development can be the first thing to be cut. This is counter-productive. It is no accident that some of the world's most successful companies also have systems in place that make them great places to work!

People are complex and unpredictable, cultures in businesses are varied and intangible, and economies in different parts of the world are in different stages of development. So, as a brilliant business strategist, how can you find a strategy for HRM? To begin, here are two things you could take a position on:

1 Find the relevant context.
2 Find the relevant action.

Find the relevant context

Is it the external environment or the internal culture?

The *external* HRM context includes the political and legal situation where your business is located, as well as population demographics (are you in an ageing population or a young one?). It also recognises the education system and macroeconomic trends of trade, development and technology.

The *internal* HRM context covers the history, culture and practices within an organisation, industry or type of business (humans transfer skill sets and cultural experience when they move from one organisation to another). Edgar Schein, an American professor who has studied organisations for many decades, developed a view that culture is found at three levels:[5]

- **Artefacts:** places, buildings, dress codes and outward symbols.
- **Espoused values:** standards, habits, norms and shared beliefs, often made explicit in brochures, rules, procedures and other visible media.
- **Basic assumptions:** the psyche of the organisation, its deeply held values, evident by implication from its actions and probably mostly invisible to those working there.

The internal context can also include an audit of the competences and capabilities within the company, which links to the resource-based view (RBV).

Find the relevant action

Do you follow others' best practice or construct your own best fit?

A **best practice** approach to HRM investigates standards to adopt or adapt in your own organisation. Very often it looks at the success stories of others and so is a bit like benchmarking very general policies for hiring, training and rewarding. Bundled together in the right combination, an organisation tries to use them as an advantage in the market. Do such advanced HR policies result in excellent companies or do excellent companies tend to result in advanced HR policies?[6] A best practice for the organisation might not be the best outcome for an individual who works there. And, if you and your competitors *all* followed the same best practice in SHRM, you would never achieve a competitive advantage.

Best fit, meanwhile, is what is known as a contingent approach (a fancy way of saying 'it depends') that you construct as a bespoke HR policy to fit your environment or your company's unique character (whichever context feels best). Best fit solutions often match the stage of development of the organisation or the stage of development the industry is in. The fit that is best will change over time and means you must constantly adapt to the unique conditions your organisation is facing. In other words, the strategic message to people is 'grow with us . . .'. By the way, no one is going to tell which of these is correct or the correct one for you. This is your job to work out or to reject and come up with your own version. But, by and large, these are the categories that most organisations use.

The sorts of future policies, systems and structures that strategic HRM can cover include:

- identifying and codifying particular skills, competences and experience needed;
- the correct learning and development needs;
- the nature of the employment relationship with its rights and responsibilities on both sides. This is partly about law and regulation, and partly about emotional commitment (sometimes also called the **psychological contract**);
- motivation and culture, empowerment, systems of reward and also of hierarchy, organisation, authority and power;
- succession planning for key staff.

Equally important for a brilliant business strategist to remember is that knowledge depends on people's engagement.

knowledge depends on
people's engagement

Strategic marketing

Marketing and strategy have a special relationship and, in fact, often speak the same language. They have a shared interest in refreshing the value proposition from the present into the future. Both are externally focused, both need people inside the organisation to be on board, and both are much harder to get right than you think.

 **brilliant** definition

Marketing

'Marketing is about identifying and meeting human and social needs.'[7]

To this brief definition you can add 'profitably' and, if you are being complete, extend 'human and social needs' beyond customers to include those of employees, suppliers and other stakeholders.

 **tip**

Marketing always starts with a customer and a need. Everything else follows from this.

What can be called a marketing activity covers a wide range of possibilities. Marketing (say marketers) is what gives purpose to processes and operations, generates income and draws on finance, and utterly depends on the talent and creativity of people. Marketing is active in the here and now, but is intensely interested in what is next and what is new. As with operations and finance, though, it is when it looks to the *future* that marketing becomes strategic.

> marketing is what gives purpose to processes and operations

The job of marketing is summarised in the 7Ps of the marketing mix:

Product: the expression of a value proposition in the eyes of your customer. A product or service is what delivers this in a tangible way.

Place: the channels and form of distribution of a product. How it reaches a customer.

Price: to you, price is revenue (every other P in this mix is a cost to you). For your customer, it is a cost.

Promotion: the communication with customers and competitors, usually seen as branding. Communication *from* customers is market research.

People: the training given to, and attitude taken towards, your employees.

Process: the management of the customer experience. Since *every* operation in the organisation can affect this, getting those wrong can damage reputation and, ultimately, the bottom line.

Physical evidence: not every service or product is tangible, so marketers work hard to create other forms of evidence that will give consumers a sense of connection.

Strategic marketing has changed to meet new challenges in recent years and will keep reinventing itself; it is the strategic marketer's job to spot trends. Some of the more pressing drivers for change are:

- **Sophisticated, high-level needs and wants:** although basic needs for food, shelter and safety are always there, the growing market for specialised social needs and personal wants is opening up new possibilities. The world's population is still growing (it will peak in around 2050), and in most places more basic needs are being met and affluence is growing. As it does, so does aspiration.

- **Emerging new technology:** this means that people and organisations (most marketing activity is business-to-business, or B2B) can search for information more easily and competitors can reach potential customers. Social media, mobile technology and internet capacity have blurred the lines of traditional marketing. If you have downloaded a copy of this book, think for a moment about all the systems and choices that have made that possible.

The fourth era of marketing

Not everybody will want or need what you are selling and you will not have the resources (or wish) to satisfy all the needs and wants of everybody out there. Somewhere in the middle is your space. To find it you need to **segment** the giant cake (probably several times), actively **target** a profitable slice of it, and then put all your mind to **positioning** your offering in the best possible light, compared to any alternatives.

In 1960, Pillsbury company executive Robert Keith declared that marketing had seen three ages.[8] The *production era* had been the first. This was all about making a profit by selling in volume, which usually worked because mass production was feeding a huge growth in consumerism. The *sales era*, when demand could easily be met by supply, saw marketers begin to look for original ways to persuade people to buy what had already been designed and made. Third came the *marketing era*, as companies listened much more carefully to find (or create, depending on your view) the needs of new consumers. The marketing era proved to be a golden period of corporate growth through competitive advantage and market share. But now comes the fourth era, which is about *relationships*. To keep customers loyal to you, you need more than clever advertising or extra fancy bells and whistles on your product. The whole organisation needs to have a market orientation, all the time.

Is it really like this, always, and wherever you go?

No. And yes.

> **No:** products, businesses and industries all go through cycles of *birth, growth, maturity* and *decline* (and *renewal*). At different times, your focus, maturity of resources and competitive position will change and evolve. You will

always be dealing with the market situation as you find it in the present.

Yes: even companies in a static period of growth know that things will change. It is the duty of the strategist to continue to create value, and achieve the vision and mission, in the future as well. Strategic marketing must tie together research and business development.

Putting it together

A brilliant business strategist understands that every business or organisation has its own way of doing things. Those in charge of setting corporate strategy must draw on their own experience and subject expertise, as well as develop new ways of seeing the world outside the company they work for. As managers, they should learn the ropes of their own business's area first *but* if they are going to be effective as strategists, they must also learn how all the different parts of a business connect and interconnect, and how others make their decisions and do their jobs.

Take another look at your answer to the question asked earlier about what it would take to disrupt your own business in the future. Can you apply some of those ideas to what is going on in your organisation at this functional level?

brilliant tip

From time to time, make appointments to go and meet the functional directors and heads in your organisation. Aim as high as you can. Ask them to explain what they do and how it links to your job.

The simplest way to struggle in the future, of course, is by not being ready for it. How quickly can your organisation mobilise?

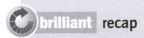 **recap**

Here is a summary of the main ideas that you can apply or bring to your own practice as a manager:

- If you are a CEO or strategic leader and you are spending your day telling others how to do their job, you are not doing yours.

- It may be art as much as a science, but knowing what value a strategic initiative will add in terms of what a business is worth is important. Use the expertise of your finance and accounting people to help work this out.

- Work that has no meaning and workplaces that provide little psychological safety – even if they have a glossy, all-singing-all-dancing HR manual to die for – are unlikely to generate strategic value.

- 'The aim of a business is to create a customer,' said Peter Drucker. Of all the drivers for strategic change, this may be the most important.

References

[1] Hubbard, E. (1911) attributed in *Items of Interest*. Vol. 33, p. 8.

[2] *Undercover Boss*. Available from: http://www.channel4.com/programmes/undercover-boss/

[3] Zander, B. (2008) 'The transformative power of classical music', TED talk. Available from: http://www.ted.com/talks/benjamin_zander_on_music_and_passion/transcript?language=en [accessed: 3 July 2015].

[4] Storey, J. (2007) 'Human resource management today: an assessment'. In Storey, J. (ed.) *Human Resource Management: A Critical Text*. London: Cengage Learning, p. 7.

[5] Schein, E. (2010) *Organizational Culture and Leadership.* 4th Ed. London: John Wiley & Sons.

[6] Spoiler alert: no one really knows!

[7] Kotler, P., Keller, K., Brady, M., Goodman, M. and Hansen, T., (2012) *Marketing Management.* 2nd Ed. Harlow: Pearson.

[8] Keith, R. (1960) 'The Marketing Revolution', *Journal of Marketing* 24(3), pp. 35–38.

CHAPTER 7

How to lead, implement change and evaluate strategy

You can accomplish anything in life, provided that you do not mind who gets the credit.

Harry S. Truman

How this chapter will help you

Leadership is the crux of successful strategy implementation, but being a strategic leader is more than pushing a plan through, come what may. A good leader knows not just when to act, but how. Complex strategic issues call for complex responses. A good leader also knows how to shut up and listen and knows that a leader without followers is not a leader. This chapter combines sensitivity in leadership, effectiveness in implementation and relevance in evaluation. It will equip you with some more of the awareness needed for a brilliant strategy.

> a leader without followers is not a leader

Introduction

An effective strategy implies its implementation. If it does not, it remains an idea in a folder gathering dust on a shelf. But strange things happen to a plan when it meets reality. Part of your role as a brilliant business strategist is to respond accordingly.

 'If you want truly to understand something, try to change it.'

Kurt Lewin[1]

It should be part of the strategist's mission to create the right atmosphere for change, but achieving this depends on two things:

1 The culture and context of the organisation.

2 *You* and your feelings about being in a leadership role.

Getting others to buy in, empowering them by listening to what they say and observing what they do, letting others have their say, and surveying what is going on outside the walls of the department or organisation – all these are leadership skills you will need to implement strategy successfully.

Leadership for strategists

Leading is a basic function of management. In fact, in the last 30 years probably more books have written about leadership than any other business or management topic. Believe it or not, no one yet has fully defined leadership; our best guess is usually a combination of different ideas and factors. In this chapter, I am going to focus on the three requirements (from amongst the many) that I believe have something to say when it comes to being a brilliant business strategist. These are shown in Figure 7.1.

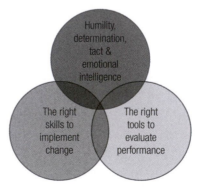

Figure 7.1 Three requirements for leadership in strategy

To have the skills and the resources, but lack emotional maturity, modesty and wisdom, results in management gains for the organisation that can only be short-lived. Such flash-in-the-pan leaders are fragile and when they leave the strategy leaves with them. Yet a well-intentioned, aware and technically skilled leader whose organisation lacks the resources needed (e.g. the right team or right materials) will be frustrated, as they will not be able to change much. At the intersection of all three (right qualities, right talents, right tools) is a powerful position for a strategist, so let us visit each requirement in more detail, starting with personal attributes.

Requirement 1: humility, determination, tact and emotional intelligence

People who act to find new ways of doing are known as **change agents.**

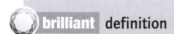 **brilliant** definition

Change agent

This is a role played by a person who is committed to bringing about a fundamental shift from current arrangements. Anyone can be a change agent when the conditions are right.

Change agents can be officially authorised: appointed to lead a transformation process. Or they can be unofficial and emerge at any level in an organisation. In anything other than a learning organisation, unofficial change agents tend to be ignored. Official or not, they are almost certain to face opposition – after all, they want to topple the status quo.

'So much of what we call management consists in making it difficult for people to work.'

Peter Drucker

Bulldozer tactics in leadership may produce spectacular results at first but usually result in a mess, with debris that someone else will have to tidy up. To effect change or implement a strategy that lasts, you need people who will listen with an open mind and who are willing to participate as partners. This is sometimes called **co-production of strategy.** No matter how well thought-through and scientific your plan is, you will need the support and belief of those around you, and you need the right people around you. This is as true for middle and lower levels of an organisation as it is at the top.

 **tip**

Leaders are not created by having an idea, they exist by having followers.

The attitude highlighted below must also be a description of you. If you cannot achieve this for yourself, how can you expect it from others?

Humility and determination

According to a 2011 *Harvard Business Review* article, you need to be an *ambidextrous* leader.[2] On the one hand, you need a *transactional* style of leadership when your job is to set up or achieve an existing goal through a combination of motivation (rewards) and positional authority. On the other hand (remember, you are ambidextrous), other contexts call for a *transformational* style, where you are exploring, experimenting, motivating and inspiring others to join you in this change.

The importance of humility to transformational leaders was a surprise finding in some well-known research by Jim Collins.[3] He studied corporations that consistently outperformed the market and found that what they all had in common was 'Level 5' leaders, as he called them. What marks them out as special is a combination of humility (often the result of reflection from a personal setback) and a very strong will or ambition.

 **definition**

Humility

This is a genuine modesty and lack of boastfulness or wish for public praise.

What this looks like in a person is:

- a quiet determination and the appeal to strong values, not personality, to motivate others;
- drive and ambition, but for the organisation first, not so much themselves. They genuinely want their successor to do better than them (many leaders do not) and are more concerned with stewardship than self-interest;
- willingness to offer praise for others for success and lack of blame for failure;
- a winner, someone who enjoys getting things done;
- unafraid of the unpleasant or unpopular if they will show positive results in the long-term;
- very high standards for the company and for those around them.

'We are the only species that follows unstable pack leaders,' says animal behaviour expert Caesar Milan, and you can contrast the list above with our usual stereotype of the corporate leader as a ruthless, domineering mover and shaker.

Tact – choosing the right style for the context you are in
Tact leads to good tactics. Tact is about dealing sensitively and appropriately with difficult issues and making the right choice in a particular context. Mike Pedler, John Burgoyne and Tom Boydell, three British management experts, spent many years investigating approaches to leadership, learning and strategy in business organisations.[4] They encountered three styles, or stances (*classical, modern* and *relational*), in organisations. Table 7.1 details each of these.

_____
tact leads to good
tactics
_____

It is the third style, the *relational* one, that I am getting at in this book. It shows nicely why strategy is such a challenging and interesting subject and why the biggest obstacle to change is often management of the politics inside an organisation making changes. For this style to work, leaders need to create trust. You cannot fake this. A recent survey in the United States showed that effective leadership is most seriously blocked by poor communication and disengagement by those in charge. 'Not recognising achievement', 'Giving unclear directions' and 'Not making time to interact face-to-face with employees' were

Table 7.1 Three stances of leadership

	Stance 1: Classical	Stance 2: Modern	Stance 3: Relational
Leadership comes from . . .	. . . personal dominance, command and control, and doing things well	. . . influence between people, winning them over and doing things better	. . . setting the right conditions for it to grow, is a collective dialogue where differences are tolerated and valued, and the aim is doing better things
The business environment is . . .	. . . uncomplicated, relatively stable	. . . changeable, but more or less predictable	. . . complex, turbulent and interconnected
Vision and strategy . . .	. . . come from those at the top, and are moved down only when top management feels it would be useful	. . . decided by those at the top after due consultation and discussion and shared with everyone to gain buy-in	. . . emergent from conversations with many opinions and stakeholders, all of whom may have legitimate visions of their own
Strategic purpose . . .	. . . is defined at the top	. . . is located at the top. Others are expected to buy into this and set their own purpose to fit in	. . . is shared, of interest to everyone and defined collectively
Strategic power . . .	. . . sits with position. The higher you are, the more power you have	. . . sits at the top, but is also delegated to operational levels to align with corporate goals	. . . is decentralised and distributed across all stakeholders, as appropriate
Strategic knowledge . . .	. . . is possessed more by those at the top than those in the middle or at the bottom	. . . is spread across the organisation but must be re-focused on achieving the purpose, as defined by the top	. . . is understood to reside in the relations between different stakeholder groups. Everyone is entitled to hold their own beliefs

Source: Pedler, M., Burgoyne, J. and Boydell, T. (2010) *A Manager's Guide to Leadership: An Action Learning Approach*. 2nd Ed. New York: McGraw-Hill, pp. 107–108. © 2010, reproduced with kind permission of McGraw-Hill Education. All Rights Reserved.

the top three complaints from middle management about those at the top. But it is not the CEO alone who should be expected to lead change. Middle managers, too, have a leadership role in strategy implementation.

brilliant tip

We are all in favour of change; until we have to change, that is. Managers who put themselves before other people, or before the values and purpose of their organisation, tend not to be good listeners.

Emotional intelligence (EI or EQ)

In the early 1980s, thanks mainly to the work of American psychologist Howard Gardner, the idea that IQ might not be the be-all and end-all of measuring intelligence landed in management training and leadership development. Gardner categorised eight intelligences (including spatial, linguistic and interpersonal) and this opened a conversation amongst management educators about whether you could measure a person's ability to read the emotional states of other people. The term **emotional intelligence** (EI) came in the mid-1990s, courtesy of Daniel Goleman, who has since written a number of books relating to EI in work and social communities.

brilliant definition

Emotional intelligence

This is the attempt to measure how adept you are at monitoring your and others' emotional states and how you use this to guide behaviours.

In plain language, EI is your ability to read people well. Whether this is a trait you are born with or a skill you can pick up, is not too clear, but the relational style, above, relies on you having it. When a concept looks this useful, it starts to look trendy; everyone wants simple explanations and quick self-measurement. I think this is missing the point. The purpose of emotional intelligence is to respect the complexity of self-discovery (in yourself and in others). Awareness of this can happen quickly (under the right circumstances), but mastery cannot be forced or quantified.

 'An emotionally intelligent manager is self-aware, is socially skilled, empathic, resilient, self-motivated and assertive, can make decisions intuitively and read other people's emotions pretty well. Basically, treats people like human beings but is open and honest enough to have the difficult, as well as the easy, conversations and, as a result, exerts a lot of influence.'

Richard Whittington, Gerry Johnson, Phyl Johnson[5]

However, EI awareness is not enough on its own. You need to combine it with the drive, passion and actions that make change happen.

Requirement 2: the right skills to implement change

The second important aspect of a leader's role in delivering strategy is the right skills in managing the process of change.

The groundwork for strategic activity generally is done a long time before any implementation actually happens. Senior management has to keep on explaining why there is a need to change and middle management must be proactive in asking for this. Without knowing *why* they should do something in a different way, or do something brand new, people will be reluctant to embrace change. If it is feasible, getting everyone together to think about (and share) the purpose of the business is ideal.

brilliant tip

Periodically asking your team (and yourself) 'What is this organisation here for?' will open debate on the aims and objectives of your business.

The feedback from this helps establish the common commitment to (or adjustment in) purpose. Another reason for asking those you work with about the essence of your business is that it helps check whether continuing to do what the company does now is sustainable or not.

brilliant questions

Is there a difference between your purpose for the organisation and your purpose for yourself? Should you take into account the purposes of all the other individuals who work there?

Change agents respond to change drivers. There are two types:

- **Internal** drivers for change have many sources, including:
  - a desire to expand the scope or geographical reach of the business;
  - an impending merger or acquisition;

- the output from research and development of new technologies, products or services;
- a requirement to control costs or reduce headcount in order to keep the business going.
- **External** drivers of change (things that force your hand) may include:
  - changes in the regulatory system affecting your industry;
  - potential *new* customers with new demands;
  - disruptive innovations to an industry;
  - political shifts, macroeconomic trends or new trade agreements;
  - moves made by key competitors or changes in influence of various stakeholders.

All the drivers listed above create movement *towards* a desired future state. All create force, but some will have more importance than others. At the same time, other forces will be acting on the organisation (from inside and out) in a way to hold you back. A great way of illustrating these competing energies is with the force-field analysis (Figure 7.2) developed by Kurt Lewin, an early pioneer of learning in organisations.[6] Quick, insightful and versatile, this is one of my favourite models in strategy.

In the force-field model, movement towards or away from a current state to a desired future outcome takes place inside a field of contradictory forces. Because some factors have more energy than others, you can give them weightings (e.g. 1 to 5). *Restraints* may also come in many shapes, sizes and degrees of importance. Resistance to change in organisations can include:

- **sunk investment:** people want the money, time and effort already invested to be earned back;
- **an attachment to old competences:** having built up strengths in one area, the whole company becomes aligned

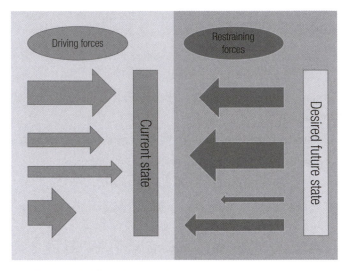

Figure 7.2 Force-field analysis of change
Source: Lewin, K. (1997) *Resolving Social Conflicts, and Field Theory in Social Science*.
Washington, DC: American Psychology Association. Reproduced with permission.

to those skills. People usually look for more of the same in
any new venture;

● **political resistance:** people will feel that change is
going to leave them worse off. No one wants to be
a loser in status, reputation or salary when change
happens;

● **being tied to a way of working:** when everyone is using
one software platform, for example, the idea of switching
to a new standard will meet with resistance, unless
handled sensitively.

For a force-field exercise to work, you must be sure about the
desired future state and honest about where you are now. The
following example draws on some work done with senior
management teams working in one part of the NHS in which
we used the force-field framework.

 **example**

Implementing mental health strategy, West London

The National Health Service (NHS) has provided free-at-point-of-contact health care in England since it was set up in 1948. It employs nearly 1.4 million staff, of whom 37,000 are managers or senior managers, and deals with 1 million patients every 36 hours. The British Government spends about 8.5 per cent of its GDP on health care, which is lower than many other advanced economies, and less than half the percentage of the United States. Total NHS expenditure will top £113 billion in 2014–15 and it will have a deficit of £617 million in this period. The UK population is growing in size, growing older in average age and becoming increasingly chronically unhealthy.

There are 209 Clinical Commissioning Groups (CCGs) in England. CCGs are responsible for planning and buying all the local health services for the population in an area. The strategic issues that commissioners deal with include funding shortfalls and changing patient demographics. CCGs must work closely with NHS England on a number of priority areas, including mental health.

'Parity of esteem' is a national ambition for mental health services to be on a par with physical health services by 2020. The NHS is under a lot of strain to deliver services, yet is committed to achieving this parity with physical health. What this means is that someone who has become mentally unwell will be able to access and have the same level of treatment as if they were physically unwell. This means that CCGs need to give equal consideration to resourcing mental health as physical health. In England there are 54 Mental Health Trusts, which provided care to 1.75 million people 2013–14.

Perinatal mental health – it is estimated that 20 per cent of women will experience perinatal mental illness. Perinatal refers to the time period from pre-conception to one year post-birth. The total long-term cost in England of all mental illness in pregnancy is approximately £8.1 billion per year. People ▷

with existing mental illness may need support from a specialist service in this time as well as those who acquire a mental illness in the perinatal period. Suicide is the number one cause of maternal death in the UK.

As part of this, Hammersmith & Fulham CCG commissioned West London Mental Health Trust (WLMHT) to develop and implement a service to meet the needs of the population. The development principles of this work were co-productive: there was an equal and reciprocal relationship between professionals, people using services, their families and their neighbours.

In September 2014, a workshop was held where the vision and the principles of the service were agreed. The commissioners wanted to ensure that no one would have to suffer alone, regardless of their level of need. The mental health and GP commissioners both disclosed mental illness that they had experienced in the perinatal period. This allowed the group to feel safe and develop a sense of everyone being in this together, and reduced any perceived hierarchy. Over a series of workshops and working groups, an integrated service was designed together (as opposed to placing patient engagement at the end of the design process). The group also aligned with maternity services, health visiting and children's centres in order to drive the agenda forward.

As CCG commissioner Clare Lyons-Collins put it, 'By stepping back from commissioners/psychiatrists/GPs being individual and by having one vision as we all were equal partners, we managed to secure funding to deliver a comprehensive service for 20 per cent of women, and education to health professionals and those in contact with new parents.'[7]

The strategic change process

Strategy suffers from being grounded in dreams and visions. Too often it stays right there. No one is more committed to the idea that strategic change is all about the actions you take and facts you manage than John Kotter. Keenly aware that most change projects fail to take root, he researched patterns amongst organisations that manage it well, eventually presenting this as an eight-step change process model (shown in Figure 7.3).

Figure 7.3 Kotter's eight-step process for leading change
Source: http://www.kotterinternational.com/our-principles/changesteps/changesteps, Kotter
International. Reproduced with permission.

In this model there are three distinct stages of leadership
required during the strategic change process – preparing the
climate, actively getting everyone involved and moving, and
following through the implementation phase. At the beginning the change agent performs the important function of
establishing a sense of urgency; a kind of shared excitement.
Of course, you have to do more than simply know the names
of these eight steps. For one thing, there are hidden reefs,
surprise traps and deadly pitfalls at each stage. For another,
meaning-making at one stage relies on feedback loops from all
the previous ones.

brilliant question

If feedback is so important in managing a change process, how would you –
as change agent - make sure those loops came back into the process?

Here are the top five reasons why change may fail to happen in strategic transformation. See if you can map any of them to Kotter's eight steps:

1 **People feel threatened and dictated to.** This is made worse when senior management dresses up a strategy fixed months ago as still open to negotiation.[8] Good strategic leadership addresses the emotional response and acknowledges everyone's legitimate feelings and emotions. Change *is* scary. People will want to know whether their jobs are at risk and whether they will be listened to in the process. Even when top management has done its sums and followed a sound logic, many strategic initiatives fail to achieve their original potential because middle managers find they have only very limited power to influence strategic issues and direction.

2 **Change agents and leaders fail to explain why the strategy is needed.** They assume everyone knows! This is a big assumption and a big mistake. Most people are busy keeping their heads above water in their jobs, so strategic leadership needs to lift their vision every now and again and get them excited about what is being planned. What is the compelling need for change? If you cannot explain that, or there is no need for change, then the implementation will fail.

3 **Strategic goals do not get translated into action.** How many times have you seen a big plan announced, only for the details to be left out and no one assigned to fix the gap?

4 **Senior management makes the big speeches to rouse the troops at the start – then disappears.** Here, strategy is considered by the top management to have been delivered before it actually has. The one resource it could contribute – being approachable – never materialises.

5 **Strategy becomes a political football in boardroom power games.** It is not usually admitted in public, but a common

reason why a strategy comes unstuck is that it becomes hopelessly entangled in a world of corporate and office politics.

As a strategic leader, which of these should you be most concerned about?

Stakeholder mapping

The territory around the strategist is made up from different groups of people, each with their own sets of interest in the outcome. These are your stakeholders.

 **definition**

Stakeholders

'Stakeholders are those individuals or groups who depend on an organisation to fulfil their own goals and on whom, in turn, the organisation depends.'[9]

Table 7.2 lists some typical categories of internal and external stakeholders.

Table 7.2   Internal and external stakeholders

Internal	External
Shareholders and investors	Financial institutions, banks, creditors
Board or executive level management	Customers
Staff (and their families)	Suppliers
You (and your family)	Competitors
	Legislators, government agencies
	Unions
	Non-governmental organisations (NGOs)
	Press, media
	The general public

Strategy leadership is as much about managing this web of relationships as it is analysing facts and figures. As you can imagine, this is a lot of juggling. What all your stakeholder groups have in common, of course, is that they consist of people (yes, even government), so your people skills will come to the fore.

---

brilliant question

Which stakeholders have *primary* importance for your organisation (i.e. their inputs are vital to your firm)?

No matter how technical or how analytical and hard-headed you want to be, you will not avoid the necessity to hold the interests of more than one group (perhaps with conflicting expectations and priorities) in your mind at once. When aluminium giant Alcoa in the 1990s embarked on a strategic implementation of lean manufacturing called the Alcoa Business System (based on the Toyota Production System), one of the central organising principles was 'people are the linchpin of the process'. By saying this they were recognising the importance of the employee stakeholder group in the outcome.

Power

Stakeholder groups vary in size, distance to or from the action, and level of influence on your actions. This creates political decisions. We often associate influence with the symbols of position in a hierarchy, but, as a strategist, you discover that it emerges from three directions:

1 **Power:** how much can a stakeholder decide to do what they want, whether you like it or not?

2 **Legitimacy:** how great is their legal or contractual claim on you?

3 **Urgency:** how important is it that they be dealt with quickly?

Map these against each other, as Ronald Mitchell has done (in Figure 7.4), and you get an intriguing way of showing where your energies should go.[10]

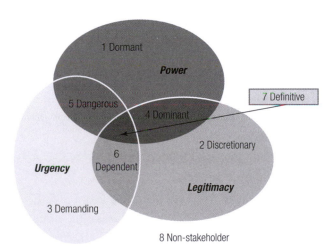

Figure 7.4 Mitchell's stakeholder mapping
Source: Mitchell, R., Agle, B. and Wood, D. (1997) 'Toward a theory of stakeholder identification and salience: Defining the principle of who and what really counts', *The Academy of Management Review* 22(4), pp. 853–886. Copyright © 1997 by Academy of Management. Reprinted with permission.

1 **Dormant** stakeholders could impose their will, but do not have the authority or the immediate need to do so. *Action: keep informed.*

2 **Discretionary** stakeholders have a claim or valid interest, but lack the authority or the need to influence. *Action: involve only when you need to.*

3 **Demanding** stakeholders have immediate need for attention, but little or no legitimacy or right to push that through. *Action: prioritise other groups first.*

4 **Dominant** stakeholders maintain both power and a legitimate claim, but not necessarily a pressing need. *Action: keep well informed.*

5 **Dangerous** stakeholders have power, because they can act independently of you, and an immediate need, but no legal or contractual legitimacy. *Action: keep an eye on, and engage with to keep happy.*

6 **Dependent** stakeholders may not have the power, but do have legitimate claim and the need to have these served quickly. *Action: manage with care, as they may interact with other stakeholders.*

7 **Definitive** stakeholders intersect all three types. *Action: full communication, all the time.*

8 **Non-stakeholders** have no effective influence. If you are taking time with these, you are damaging your strategy implementation.

 **question**

Who is in charge?

That may sound like a stupid question to ask, but implementation goes a lot more smoothly when everyone knows where authority and responsibility lie. There is no single right answer for this. Different organisations, with different cultures, dealing with different strategic issues have different responses. Is authority devolved? Is it at the centre? Is it distributed to teams?

Requirement 3: the right tools to evaluate performance

The third part of strategic delivery concerns evaluating what has been implemented. Does strategic planning pay? Without the right measures, you will never know (even *with* the right measures, with some kinds of change project you may still never know).

First things first – what are you going to measure to evaluate your strategy? To simplify this, break it into three steps, each of which generates its own set of questions.

---

brilliant questions

● Step 1: Be clear about your strategic issues, choices, chosen direction and decisions: Were the objectives ambitious enough to address the issue, but not too big that they over-stretched the organisation? Was the urgent need for change accepted? Were all relevant stakeholders fully identified and briefed?

● Step 2: Agree early on the diagnostic measurements that you plan to make during the implementation phase: Did every objective have an appropriate form of measurement? How often was information fed back into the process? How was data collected and shared?

● Step 3: Agree on the most important measurements of performance against plan: what were the right measurements of performance for *this* strategic implementation? If successful, what does the change look like? What new behaviours or what new processes? What was missed?

Evaluating strategy

Before I get into details of some of the main methods used in evaluation of strategy, it is worth learning a bit about the possibilities of a good **benchmarking** policy as part of your toolkit for strategic leadership.

 **brilliant** definition

Benchmarking

This is a way of evaluating existing, and discovering potential new, best practices by studying how one or more organisations from other industries handle similar issues.

This is a definition of best-in-class benchmarking. You stand to learn more about your own assumptions when you deliberately move away from your own business area to see how a similar type of goal or objective is achieved elsewhere. If you benchmark within your own industry, you will start to find and (probably) adopt standard practices. Benchmarking can also be *retrospective,* comparing your own performance over a period of time.

brilliant tip

If you are undertaking a benchmarking exercise to evaluate your organisation's strategy, try contacting organisations in as many contrasting business sectors as you can. In return, they can learn from you.

Benchmarking, especially if it is done with an open mind, can be a good way to set up meaningful forms of measurement, and targets for performance, during a strategy implementation and change process, but it can also be over-used and, if you copy what your rivals are doing, it will be more difficult to attain competitive advantage.

Key performance indicators (KPIs) are a way of quantifying outputs. They normally include measures of productivity, efficiency and quality in the use of time, money and talent. They can also be financial indications of value creation or competitive positioning. If you work in a highly-regulated industry or in a large, multi-division or multi-business business, KPIs are part of your world (you may be sick

> a good KPI is a means to an end

of them!). It certainly can feel that you exist only to manage a target and there is a real danger of forgetting the bigger picture. For business strategists, though, a good KPI is a means to an end, not an end in itself.

brilliant tip

Be wary of choosing your KPIs from a standardised list. They should be agreed through discussion and written in plain language.

There are a million possible variables you could measure – many of them financial or numeric – but only a few will speak to the strategic issue you (or your organisation) originally identified. Aligning KPIs to corporate strategy is the job of business strategy.

Balanced scorecard

The balanced scorecard (see Figure 7.5) is a way of acknowledging that indicators of performance are not always tangible or countable. It was developed by Harvard (where else?) professors

Figure 7.5 Kaplan and Norton's balanced scorecard
Source: Kaplan, R.S. and Norton, D.P. (1996) 'Using the balanced scorecard as a strategic management system', *Harvard Business Review* 74(1), January-February, pp. 75–85. Reprinted by permission of *Harvard Business Review*. Copyright © 1996 by the Harvard Business School Publishing Corporation, all rights reserved.

Robert Kaplan and David Norton in 1992 and versions of it are used in many organisations around the world.[11]

The four aspects are:

1 **Internal business process:** straightforward metrics to diagnose issues with material aspects of a strategy. Quality and operational KPIs are best designed by the management and teams actually delivering them.

2 **Organisational capacity for learning:** the accelerating impact of technology and information on a business makes measuring this absolutely vital for evaluating the success of a strategy. As with the internal processes, these need to be constructed in dialogue with those who are involved in the various systems used, but the strategy leadership team must create the right conditions of trust for this to happen.

3 **Customer/stakeholder satisfaction:** negative feedback can have immediate and damaging impact, so this is front and centre as a scorecard element, alongside measures from other key stakeholders.

4 **Financial measures:** traditional performance metrics remain important. When all is said and done, most managers are concerned with the health of the financial bottom line.

 **tip**

Strategy evaluation should be iterative and feedback from KPIs should be used to inform the strategic decision-making process as you go.

The triple bottom line

Another way of evaluating strategy that is closer to the question of stewardship is the **triple bottom line** (see Figure 7.6), which was developed by John Elkington at around the same time as the balanced scorecard, emerging from discussions on how to achieve United Nations development goals.[12]

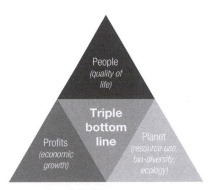

Figure 7.6 John Elkington's triple bottom line
Source: Adapted from Elkington, J. (1999) *Cannibals with Forks: Triple Bottom Line of the 21st Century Business.* Minnesota: Capstone.

The financial bottom line of profit and loss is a predictable measure of the strategic imperative to create economic value, and the inclusion of a measure of human quality of life echoes some of the aims of the balanced scorecard. What is new here is consideration of the positive or negative effects of human activity and commercial growth on the planet or biosphere.

The triple bottom line creates aims for business. The tension

___

the triple bottom line creates aims for business

___

between 'people' and 'profits' needs to be *equitable*; between 'planet' and 'people' it must be *sustainable* and *manageable*.

Putting it all together: the Cynefin framework

David Snowden has introduced a sense-making model (see Figure 7.7) for leaders to recognise that decision-making resides in many different places (cynefin, pronounced *ki-NE-vin*, means habitat or place in Welsh).[13] As a manager, you start in the centre – in what always feels to you like *disorder*. You are yet to decide what sort of territory an issue lives in (e.g. is it open or closed?). Rather than start with a neat 2x2 framework to impose on your issue, you question the data to show you where that particular issue needs to emerge in the framework. Then you act accordingly.

Many management tasks are typical of *simple* systems. Cause and effect are visible and results predictable and repeatable. Decision making here can be part of an existing frame, such as following **best practice.** Best practice suggests there is only one right way.

When a system is *complicated,* cause and effect are still easy to identify, but the solution may first require you to analyse and process data before acting. Decision making is more a matter of *good practice.* The difference between that and best practice is that you may find more than one possible solution that will work. The right way may not be the only way.

Complex systems, meanwhile, have cause and effect only in hindsight. At the time, there are too many unpredictable inputs

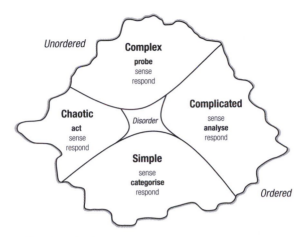

Figure 7.7 The Cynefin framework
Source: Snowden D.J. and Boone M.E. (2007) 'A leader's framework for decision making', *Harvard Business Review* 85(11), November, pp. 69–76. Reprinted by permission of *Harvard Business Review*. Copyright © 2007 by the Harvard Business School Publishing Corporation all rights reserved.

for you to predict outcomes. What is causing your issue may be part of a deeper and much less obvious pattern. You must carry out experiments to probe the situation, responding to the various kinds of feedback you get along the way. This results in **novel** and **new practice.**

Sometimes a company gets itself mixed up in a *chaotic* system, on purpose. This is usually for a goal such as innovation, and therefore only for a short time. If you were to find yourself in chaos unexpectedly, then the correct practice is to *act,* and quickly. This is a bit like getting a hand-held GPS device to work – you have to move a bit for it to get some data to find out where you are.

---

brilliant tip

You can take another person only as far along as you have gone yourself. If you want to lead and implement change as a strategist, you need to start with your own intention.

The advantage of this framework is that it reminds us that different types of situation call for different types of action from you. But remember, you always begin in the *disorder* category –

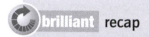
different types of
situation call for
different types of action

but you do so using whatever lens or bias you have been trained to think in. Snowden points out that you can cross from one zone to another without too much trouble – except one. The move from the simple zone to the chaotic is a cliff; rigid and over-simplified reactions in an organisation can be what send the whole system into a crisis.

brilliant recap

Here is a summary of the main ideas that you can apply or bring to your own practice as a manager:

- Being a change agent in strategy is a leadership role. Change agents can be appointed or they can emerge, but they all need to demonstrate some key qualities to succeed.

- A strategic leadership role also needs the right technical and social skills of management to oversee and implement a process. You will face opposition and sometimes that opposition is right, so flexibility is key.

- There is no point working out and implementing a strategy if you have no way of knowing whether it was successful. The third task of a strategic leader is finding out what is worth measuring in evaluation.

References

[1] Attributed in Tolman, C.W. (1995) *Problems of Theoretical Psychology*. Coventry: International Society for Theoretical Psychology, p. 31.
[2] Tushman, M.L., Smith, W. K. and Binns, A. (2011) 'The ambidextrous CEO', *Harvard Business Review* 89(6), pp. 74–80.

[3] Collins, J.C. (2001) *Good to Great: Why Some Companies Make the Leap . . . and Others Don't.* New York: Collins Business.

[4] Pedler, M., Burgoyne, J. and Boydell, T. (2010) *A Manager's Guide to Leadership: An Action Learning Approach.* 2nd Ed. New York: McGraw-Hill, pp. 107–108.

[5] Johnson, G., Whittington, R. and Johnson, P., 'How intelligent are we about emotional intelligence?', White Paper. Available from: http://www.strategyexplorers.com/whitepapers/ [accessed: 29 June 2015].

[6] Lewin, K. (1947) 'Frontiers in group dynamics II. Channels of group life; social planning and action research', *Human Relations* 1(2), pp. 143–53.

[7] Case material compiled from NHS Confederation. Available from: http://www.nhsconfed.org/resources/key-statistics-on-the-nhs and email correspondence with CGC staff

[8] The everyday management equivalent to this is the classic line, 'My door is always open'.

[9] Johnson, G., Scholes, K. and Whittington, R. (2007) *Exploring Corporate Strategy: Text and Cases.* Harlow: FT Prentice Hall, p. 179.

[10] Mitchell, R., Agle, B. and Wood, D., (1997) 'Toward a theory of stakeholder identification and salience: defining the principle of who and what really counts', *Academy of Management Review* 22(4), pp. 853–866.

[11] Kaplan, R.S. and Norton, D.P. (1996) 'Using the balanced scorecard as a strategic management system', *Harvard Business Review* 74(1), January–February, pp. 75–85.

[12] Elkington, J. (1999) *Cannibals with Forks: The Triple Bottom Line of the 21st Century Business.* Minnesota: Captsone.

[13] https://www.youtube.com/watch?v=N7oz366X0–8

PART 3

Strategic thinking in a changing world

I refuse to answer that question on the grounds that I don't know the answer.

Douglas Adams

We do not know for sure what is going to happen. We can make educated guesses, but the future is inherently and creatively formed by us *in the present*. Because we can act on our vision, our present thoughts do, indeed, set up a future. Human *agency* (the capacity to act on our choices) is what has got us to where we are, for better or for worse. We *can* make a difference, within certain limits, and only some of what happens in the future will depend on how it is shaped by us. We understand more clearly than we did 10 or 20 years ago that we live in an open system, not a closed one, where our actions produce unintended consequences as well as intended ones.

In management and in business, what connects purpose and agency to the future is strategy. Are we getting this right? This is a big question. Do we need a different definition of strategy, with different premises, values and assumptions, for the future?

If we do, then it must address how we combine thought and action. So, Chapter 8 is about bringing an action learning approach to the slippery, strategic issues you or your organisation will face in the future, and Chapter 9 brings *you* back into the equation for transformative change by challenging how you think about strategy and how you think about yourself.

CHAPTER 8

The purpose and future of strategy

Why, then the world's mine oyster.

Shakespeare, *The Merry Wives of Windsor,* Act II, Scene ii

How this chapter will help you

Strategy is forward-looking. This begs a series of questions not about *what* we think – but *how*. What kind of thinking will we need in the future business environment? What kind of action? What kind of responsibility will you hold, personally, for making this happen? In this chapter you will find three responses to such questions, with examples and ideas for your practice.

Introduction

Once upon a time, the definition of **corporate social responsibility** (CSR) was that it is a manager's corporate responsibility, within the law, to make as much profit as possible.[1] Later, awareness of social issues and the environmental impact of globalised trade placed corporate philanthropy (being a good citizen) in the company report and sometimes on the balance sheet. Companies began investing in the reduction of harmful effects and waste products – but the economic growth/profit imperative remained a manager's first consideration. Under the surface, it has often remained business as usual.

In April 2010, an oil rig called Deepwater Horizon exploded and sank in the waters of the Gulf of Mexico, causing the deaths of 11 employees and leading to 3.19 million barrels of oil spilling into the sea before the well was finally sealed, 5 months later. The incident severely impacted the economy in the southern US states and devastated the marine and coastal ecosystem. The oil was dispersed, but is still damaging the environment, as pollutants and clear-up chemicals have entered the food chain.

In the inquests and litigation in the years since, blame and accountability has consistently been placed at the door of the rig owner, BP, and the subcontractors that operated it. In 2012, BP was convicted on 11 felony counts (the company was already on probation for several other corporate manslaughter charges when the Deepwater Horizon incident happened) and fined $4.5 billion. In July 2015, the company agreed to pay $18.7 billion in final settlement to the US Government and other claimants, with payment spread over 18 years and set against tax and future revenue. Though the largest such payment in US corporate history, it was considerably less than originally sought by the US Government.[2] Since 2010, BP has set aside a total of $54 billion for charges related to Deepwater Horizon. No senior manager has been charged with criminal activity in connection with the events leading up to or following the spill. Following the 2015 settlement, BP is currently planning new exploration in the Gulf of Mexico.

🌟 brilliant questions

This has, undoubtedly, been a difficult period for BP. Were its problems caused by its vision and mission? Was it following the wrong strategy? The wrong leadership? Poor tactics? Plain bad luck? How would you go about analysing these issues?

Transformation needs thought. If thinking does not inform action, then businesses *stagnate*. The trouble is that a typical middle manager's role is to act without constantly questioning why. 'Get it done' is usually the subtext from the levels above.

If actions are carried out thoughtlessly or too rigidly, businesses become *chaotic*. Either way, we have a problem. Perhaps you sometimes see evidence of this in your organisation, too.

 'We make the road by walking.'

Spanish proverb

As a brilliant business strategist, and as you walk along the road made by your organisation and its environment, here are three trends to help unlock future value creation:

1 Purpose-led transformation.

2 Values as the basis of progress.

3 Thoughtful action.

1 Purpose-led transformation

Purpose drives what we do. This is a modern human constant. But how this drive gets expressed by us changes over time. For example, spot the differences between these two public statements from US conglomerate GE. Here is the company summing itself up in 2015:

GE . . . imagines things others don't, builds things others can't and delivers outcomes that make the world work better. GE brings together the physical and digital worlds in ways no other company can. In its labs and factories and on the ground with customers, GE is inventing the next industrial era to move, power, build and cure the world.[3]

Actually, this is inspiring stuff. Now compare it to the company's headline statement in its 2007 annual report:

GE is a reliable growth company. We have positioned ourselves to invest and deliver in the most challenging of global economic environments. We have valuable leadership businesses that are positioned to capitalize on global trends. Our organic growth capabilities and disciplined financial execution prepare a strong leadership team to deliver each and every day. This is your GE.

What has changed, do you think? Are the differences you see ones of purpose, strategy or tactics? GE is currently moving away from generating income from its finance business, GE capital (to be reduced to 25 per cent of its portfolio). The language used reflects a change in emphasis from financial return to leadership in industrial infrastructure and innovation in new technology.

 **question**

When GE talks about outcomes delivering a better world, is it moving beyond the now familiar script of CSR?

An exciting new wave of CSR is emerging in the 21st century. Responsibility is slowly being moved to the heart of strategic performance, at least on a par with profitability. No longer a 'nice-to-have', profit and purpose are inter-connected. It is not so much that it would be nice to have both, it is more that you cannot have one without the other. Global consulting company EY has defined itself as a purpose-led company since 2012. Purpose for EY is 'an aspirational reason for being that is grounded in humanity and inspires action.'[4]

 **example**

EY Beacon Institute

To keep pace with change, organisations must continually transform themselves. Innovation, transformation and good business practice are nothing new, but the ethical and governance questions raised by the global financial crash of 2008 and the unpredictable social and ecological consequences of short-term economic growth have led some to re-examine the link between practice and purpose.

Launched in 2015 at the annual Davos meeting in Switzerland, the EY Beacon Institute is a collaboration of thought leaders from business and education. It unites its community members, drawn from entrepreneurs, practitioners, global CEOs and leading academics, in a series of open forums and research activities aimed at framing the business case for an evolution of our understanding of purpose in innovation and future prosperity development.

At the Davos meeting, five trends emerged:[5]

1   An evolving view of the corporation's role increasingly emphasises the corporation as a partner for societal well-being.

2   The corporate dialogue on purpose is louder and changing.

3   Executives are using a common language of purpose to engage stakeholders.

4   Purpose can be a lever, driving innovation and transformation for growth.

5   There is an implementation gap: purpose is underleveraged to drive transformation.

Each represents exciting avenues for enquiry, but also a challenge to the Institute itself. Having set off on the journey in the Alps with high hopes – and high-profile endorsement – purpose-led transformation may still have a mountain to climb to make this a reality. The quest for a sustainable growth strategy has, in the past, focused corporations almost entirely on the bottom line. Yet the goal is never attained. Now that purpose is back in the frame – and is inclusive of social well-being and sustainable global economic development – the real work begins.

The implementation gap (the last of the five Beacon Institute trends) is what much of this book has been about. As a brilliant business strategist, the gap between intention of strategy and its implementation is where you need to apply your critical thinking skills and self-awareness.

Finding wider purpose in change is a challenge, so here are three brilliant tips to help:

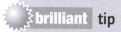 **tip**

> When you set strategy, do not evaluate policies by how much they minimise harm, rather by to what extent they explicitly promote well-being.

Does this mean reinventing your business? Not necessarily, though it might do. Depending on what else is going on in the corporate environment, it is quite possible that purpose-led strategy is a (temporary) source of competitive advantage.

brilliant tip

> The involvement of everyone concerned is essential, otherwise they are empty words. Meaning-making is collaborative.

Walk the talk. Mean it yourself. This is the only way to attract followers. If you do not already feel this way, then perhaps strategic management is not for you.

brilliant tip

> Focus on innovation only when it is in line with purpose. Change for the sake of change can be as damaging as keeping everything the same, all the time.

I love the chaotic and the tangential in my own work; a teaching process hijacked by a random thought or creative idea can lead to incredible things, but I can also see that there has to be a balance with pragmatism. The best guides on where to draw the line will be your self-awareness and your understanding of purpose-led action.

2 Values as the basis of progress

A long time ago, a younger version of me was earning some extra cash working nights behind the bar in a cramped and crowded subterranean live music venue in Central London. In its early days, the music venue had championed independent and breakthrough bands and both the club and the associated restaurant at street level were generally full and very profitable for the owners. The owners had told its managers to increase revenues. There were numerous practices designed to do this, many at the expense of the customers. Beer on tap in the bar was not as profitable as selling the bottled lagers, and the venue's management would instruct us not to sell draught beer (we had to say there was a technical fault) until they had hit their target for the more expensive bottle sales. We were powerless to object. This example is small and personal, but the point is that this flow from the top had made liars of us all – a phenomenon more common in organisations and business than we often like to admit.

Many years later, and the business school where I work is fond of a phrase much favoured by one of its founders, WHSmith: 'Character and integrity are as important as capability in a manager'.[6] Saying it does not require character and integrity, but meaning it – and acting accordingly – does. Integrity, which means being honest and principled, as well as in unity with your surroundings, speaks to our *values*.

Values

These express the 'why' in our lives. They are enduring expressions of the standards or guides we use to judge our own and other people's behaviour. Collectively established and individually expressed, they form the basis for our beliefs and the rules on how to live life.

A recent white paper from the Center for Creative Leadership revealed how integrity is an important asset to have in senior management.[7] Interestingly, they also found that it is not such an important requirement for success in middle management, where your ability to get on with other people is more important. A promotion may therefore be the first time that managers are faced with the consequences of consistency and principles in what they do.

In 2001, US cyclist Lance Armstrong appeared in a TV advertisement for Nike in which he stated, 'this is my body, and I can do whatever I want to it'. A bold rebuttal to his critics at the time, subsequent revelations and confessions as to the widespread use of banned performance-enhancing drugs during his career give pause for thought.

In January 2013 Armstrong finally admitted in public to systematic cheating over much of the course of his career.[8]

What have values got to do with strategy in the future? Everything. Senior managers need a moral compass to form corporate strategy because their decisions will affect the quality of life of many other people and may have long-lasting consequences. Middle managers need awareness of them *before* they reach senior levels because values are the factor most associated with company performance.

 **example**

Johnson & Johnson's Credo

When Regulatory Affairs Director Jo Ann Vassallo decided to move on from her previous job, she knew she was looking for an employer with values, integrity and respect for staff. In the middle of her MBA, she wanted her next career move to be a significant one. That is when she was approached by Johnson & Johnson (JnJ). She had heard about their commitment to ethics and wondered whether the company actually lived up to its image.

In her interview, she was delighted when the discussion did not just focus on *her* attitude and work ethic, but flowed in the other direction. She was given the opportunity to ask the same questions back, and ended up having a long, detailed and honest discussion about the part the Credo plays in the day-to-day life of a JnJ employee. She was encouraged to find that the Credo truly serves to guide JnJ decision making. She felt motivated and assured that she would work in a place where she felt respected and safe to learn. The opportunity to leave a personal and professional legacy was evident to her.

So, what is the JnJ Credo? Written over 70 years ago by the then head of the company and a son of the founder, Robert Wood Johnson, it was shaped by experience of the Great Depression. Johnson led with what we would now call a core sense of corporate social responsibility. In 1943, he presented the Credo to the board before the family company went public, to make sure that these values would guide growth and profitability in the organisation. This is the document:

We believe our first responsibility is to the doctors, nurses and patients, to mothers and fathers and all others who use our products and services. In meeting their needs everything we do must be of high quality. We must constantly strive to reduce our costs in order to maintain reasonable prices. Customers' orders must be serviced promptly and accurately. Our suppliers and distributors must have an opportunity to make a fair profit. ▶

We are responsible to our employees, the men and women who work with us throughout the world. Everyone must be considered as an individual. We must respect their dignity and recognize their merit. They must have a sense of security in their jobs. Compensation must be fair and adequate, and working conditions clean, orderly and safe. We must be mindful of ways to help our employees fulfill their family obligations. Employees must feel free to make suggestions and complaints. There must be equal opportunity for employment, development and advancement for those qualified. We must provide competent management, and their actions must be just and ethical.

We are responsible to the communities in which we live and work and to the world community as well. We must be good citizens – support good works and charities and pay our fair share of taxes. We must encourage civic improvements and better health and education. We must maintain in good order the property we are privileged to use, protecting the environment and natural resources.

Our final responsibility is to our stockholders. Business must make a sound profit. We must experiment with new ideas. Research must be carried on, innovative programs developed and mistakes paid for. New equipment must be purchased, new facilities provided and new products launched. Reserves must be created to provide for adverse times. When we operate according to these principles, the stockholders should realize a fair return.[9]

The JnJ Credo is a valiant attempt to record on paper (it is even written in stone at the company's headquarters) the importance of the responsible exercise of influence and power. Not for the first time in the book, it is an example of principled leadership starting with the right person who makes followers of those around them. Managers rely on their authority and influence to get things done, so you are not going to get very far as a strategist without knowing how to exercise influence and work with power.[10]

Organisational power

If you are looking for a can of worms to open amongst strategists, try a conversation on the relevance of power in management and change. Most of the big names in strategy prefer to keep fairly quiet about it – power is assumed as a given and is not up for discussion. Organisational power can easily creep beyond the usual rules of competitive positioning and engagement. A merger or an acquisition could be a legitimate economic move to build or firm up a market position, or it could be a loss-making tactic deliberately done to thwart or prevent rivals. Power is sometimes another way of saying the ends justify the means.

 **example**

Google's Nest egg

In January 2014, Nest, a smart hub producer at the forefront of the internet of things, was bought by Google for $3.2 billion. Nest develops Web 3.0 (where gadgets start talking to each other over the internet) thermostats used in automated home heating systems. Using Google cash, Nest set about acquiring various companies it had previously been in alliance or co-development with. In October 2014, Nest bought innovative Colorado start-up Revolv, producers of a hub system that could have rivalled Nest's own plans.[11]

In August 2015, Google announced a corporate reorganisation, launching as a conglomerate with the creation of a holding company, Alphabet, to manage the corporate strategy of seven separate companies, including Nest.

Was Nest merely being sensible, acquiring some excellent know-how and synergy while it could? Or was it using its new-found muscle too aggressively, crushing anyone else who might threaten its product? Was the Nest/Revolv deal a part of Google's bigger strategy?

A CEO faces uncertainty with every strategic decision she makes and must navigate a web of regulation, competing stakeholder interests (not just shareholders) and public or personal scrutiny of their morals, ethics or governance. Levels of complexity and politics increase when multiple agencies are drawn together, as happens with the oil producers of OPEC, deregulated energy supply in the UK, the manoeuvring and alliances of rival airlines . . . and so on.[12] Some business models, such as cooperatives, business societies and employee partnerships, are keenly aware of the values-based premises that brought them into being. These deliberately diffuse the power-play aspect of competitor markets without compromising the objective to remain viable and profitable (think of Waitrose, part of the John Lewis Partnership, as an example[13]).

Personal power

If you are a strategist, you cannot avoid spending (at least) some of your time in the interplay of interests inside your organisation. Personal power may have three foundations:

1 **Position:** 'Do it because I am the boss and I say so.'

   Your influence is embodied in the role you are playing in a hierarchy of command and control. Positional power means that the actors may change, but the performance can carry on. Positional power brings with it the right to use reward or punishment to get your way.

2 **Expertise:** 'Do it because I am the expert and I know so.'

   Your influence comes from the fact that you have specialist or scarce knowledge that is valuable to the achievement of a goal. This is also known as thought leadership, and is associated with the use of respect or influence to get your way. Many people who work in matrix organisations have only this to rely on. Connection power is similar and comes from the influence gained by the network you have built around you.

3 **Moral high ground:** 'Do it because it is the right thing to do.' Your influence on others is exerted by appealing to a higher set of values or beliefs. If these are ones the organisation stands to benefit from, then it is much easier to use.

brilliant questions

Think about key people in your life that have influence over you. Do you see these different forms mentioned above? What kinds of influence do *you* have over the people in your life? Are there any other types of personal power?

Personal power is often assumed to be a function of being a leader, and something you either have or you do not. Just be slightly careful. If you think power is a force, like energy, then you will be using a very different belief system than if you think power is a relationship, where information is more important than force. How you act and whether your actions are wise ones will depend on how you think.

3 Strategy as thoughtful action

By now, you should understand that to be an effective strategist you will always have to strike a balance. Several balances, actually. The first is between *managing* and *leading.* Leadership is the sexier of the two

to be an effective strategist you will always have to strike a balance at the moment but, as Henry Mintzberg reminds us, this is misleading:

 'Much of the work that can be programmed in an organization need not concern its managers directly; specialists can do it. That leaves the managers with much of the messy stuff – the intractable problems, the complicated connections.'

Henry Mintzberg[14]

In my opinion, leading and managing are only two sides of the same the coin; both are about making things happen and both need other people to help. To Mintzberg's list of intractable problems that may be unique to leading, however, I would add *visioning what is absent*.

**brilliant** tip

Seeing what is not yet there is the art in crafting a good strategy.

The second balancing act is between *stability* and *change*. We talk a lot about change, but change is literally meaningless without a reference to stability. If the *only* colour in the world were green, we would have no word for the colour green. If *everything* was changing, *all* the time, we would not know what change was. Change *is* noticeable and creates contrast, but that is because most things in our lives remain relatively constant.

> change is meaningless without a reference to stability

The goal of a mature organisation is to continue in existence. Oddly, the best way to keep that goal real might be by being able to change and reinvent what the organisation does.[15] This is quite natural. In business, Nokia began life in 1865 and has been wood miller, rubber goods and tyre manufacturer, electricity generator, cable and wire producer, and maker of consumer electrical goods, military equipment, digital switching systems, personal computers, and mobile telephony (which was the one that sent the company worldwide). It has continued to trade through the ups and downs, mergers, acquisitions, start-ups, divestments and location switches, yet not one person who founded Nokia or worked for it at the start is still alive, and none of its current products or services resembles its original offerings. Despite this, we are not confused about what Nokia is. As with the paradox in Greek mythology of the Ship of Theseus, change and stability can have one identity.[16]

 **tip**

As a strategic manager, when you grasp the idea of change, you are holding a magnet that has stability at its other pole. They are interconnected; the cause of one is the cause of the other.

Finally, there is a third balance, between *action* and *thinking*. Skilled players in strategic leadership can link action and thought in a continuous cycle. Action is data gathering; a way to inform thinking or test a hunch, with a huge amount of hit and miss (which is a polite way of saying managers must fail in order to succeed).

Strategy as 'wicked problems'

All management is about solving the challenge posed by problems. Value creation is a problem – it is not going to happen by itself without your input (unless you know something that the rest of us have missed!). The types of problem you may face fall, roughly, into three categories:

1 **Fire-fighting:** an issue flares up and if it is mission-critical, it will get immediate attention. There is little time for thought and not much point in planning or involving too many other people in decision making. Just get the problem under control.

2 **Projects and plans:** many objectives, goals or new ventures may be complex but, on the whole, any problems encountered are the sort you would expect to crop up. Many variables are known and the plan may have extra resources that can be brought in to complete the project or objective, as specified. The goal itself is not in question, just the best route to solving the puzzle (maps are always out of date, so it is still easy to get lost).

3 **Wicked problems:** these are different. They are problems that do not have a simple answer waiting to be worked out like an algorithm. Nor can you rely on past experience. Nothing works. A wicked problem has a high degree of uncertainty about its causes, context and outcome. There is no rule-book to apply. In fact, applying past experience will not work because those habits that the organisation has learnt are often also part of the wicked problem. You may actually need to unlearn some things.

Strategic issues are rarely organised and often will take the appearance of wicked problems. You know you have one if:

- **it is hard to express:** it cannot easily be written down in a statement, or quickly and neatly explained to those around you (as you might brief an ordinary work problem);
- **there is no finite end point:** in fact, there may be no 'there' to get to (at least, not in the same way as a project or a business target);

- **there is some element of dilemma:** it is a dilemma when you have more than one possible solution and each has something undesirable about it;
- **the stakes are high:** not just for the organisation but for you, too. You cannot afford not to take responsibility for your actions and decisions. You have to act. Strategists like to remind themselves of the expression 'no one is coming', because with a wicked problem there is no cavalry waiting to save you;
- **it is complex:** defined by seeing what it is part of, rather than what bits it is made up of. A wicked problem seems to change shape every time you look at it and solutions may generate all sorts of unintended consequences.

Many organisations, however, do not treat their strategic issues this way.

 'The *problem* is the domain of the leader; unlike the *puzzle*, it is charged with unanswerable questions, as well as unfathomable ones.'

Reg Revans[17]

Dedicated and talented middle managers are pivotal to strategic success. If this describes you, then you will know that the modern pace of work is unrelenting. Your job is to interpret to those lower down the decisions from above and decide what information goes back up. Email means the workplace stalks you at home and on your weekends. Meetings eat up your time without letting you digest what has been said (or unsaid) in any meaningful way. Fighting fires, simultaneously worrying about the office politics, keeping your customer happy and keeping your business unit running whilst hitting every target – it is exhausting! And your reward for solving one thing is to be given another . . . under this duress you get used to making decisions starved of time and information.

When it comes to strategy, however, problems tend not to have one simple or convenient solution or outcome. You need time, and a space, to think. What you really need is a space to challenge your own assumptions alongside other people who are not trying to impose their own solution. Enter action learning.

Action learning

Action learning (AL) is a process first developed by a British academic, Reg Revans, in the 1940s and 50s. Revans' starting point was the realisation that 'there is no learning without action, and no (sober and deliberate) action without learning.'[18]

 **brilliant** definition

Action learning

This is a process which involves working on real challenges, using the knowledge and skills of a small group of people combined with skilled questioning, to reinterpret old and familiar concepts and produce fresh ideas.

Action Learning Associates website[19]

AL is a powerful way of harnessing the collaborative power of a group (or set) in service of a difficult problem held by one of its members. This participative enquiry in management has echoes in the business models of the original Quaker businesses, such as Cadbury, Rowntree and Barclays bank, and in fact an action learning set is not restricted to generating ideas and action at work, it is also definitely a space for you to develop yourself – to question your own assumptions and frames for experience.

'Learning has to be equal to or faster than the rate of change.'

Reg Revans

The whole organisation has to keep up with, or exceed, the pace of change in the environment. That sounds remarkably similar to the challenge for strategy described by many in other parts of the book.

 **tip**

The formula for action learning is:

$$L = P + Q$$

(L stands for learning, P for programmed knowledge, or all the things you have learnt, and Q is for insightful questions.)

There is never one right way forward (if it were *that* easy, the consultants would get it right all the time), so insightful questioning by other set members is what makes this method really useful in strategy. An **action learning set** is a small group of people (all must be volunteers), preferably who work in different sectors and for different companies. The set contracts to meet over a fixed period and to support each other in addressing difficult-to-define personal and professional challenges. They may use a facilitator or manage themselves. In a set:

> there is never one right way forward

● each person personally takes ownership of a real challenge. The problem faced must be one that has proved resistant to being solved by usual methods. In short, you need to be genuinely stuck;

- the owner of the issue must acknowledge that they may be part of the problem and that the problem is part of them. Personal development is part of the action learning process;
- the group does not create new options for action for the issue holder;
- there must be action based on the insights gained. Results of action are fed back into further meetings for reflection.

Do not over-think this as a process. Try it out. Act in order to gain data and insight.

 'Never doubt that a small group of thoughtful, committed citizens can change the world. Indeed, it is the only thing that ever has.'

Margaret Mead, American cultural anthropologist

Action learning can help reveal what is going on in your competitive environment and help you explain your organisation's reactions to this. It does this by raising awareness of a problem through iterative sessions, over a period of time, of insightful questioning. Between meetings, it is very important that there is both further reflection and action. The action is key to change and is what enriches the reflection.

Let us pause for moment:

What is strategy for, again?

I have talked more about being clear on purpose *in* strategy and not so much about the purpose *of* strategy. What's it for? What does it achieve? Henry Mintzberg has summed up four mainstream beliefs (each with its own advantages and limitations):

1 **'Strategy sets direction'**: it is a plan of action; a route to a destination. But this can make us blind to hidden dangers along the way, especially if we think 'there' must be reached at all costs.

2 **'Strategy focuses effort'**: it is a flag to rally the troops. Then everyone can pull together and do things more efficiently. But, what if the generals in charge have missed something? Can anyone challenge them?

3 **'Strategy defines the organisation'**: it is our shorthand for sense-making. Strategy provides evidence of boundaries and tells us who we are. But our picture may be too simple to capture the reality.

4 **'Strategy provides consistency'**: when everything else looks uncertain, strategy provides an order and logic over time. We can then organise our actions. But our self-image may be out of date and this approach can squash creativity.[20]

brilliant question

If someone came along tomorrow and removed your entire business, is the demand for what you do so necessary that your organisation would have to be built all over again?

What assumptions about the world were needed to come up with the four statements above? What if the world is not like our assumptions? Then we would be defining the wrong challenges for ourselves and our organisations. By now, you may be happy holding more than one of these as correct, or at least valid in certain contexts, and this itself is a really good sign of a strategic competence. What is more, you may have realised that there are many other ways of cutting the world up into pieces to understand it. And here is another thought . . . by slicing up strategy in these ways, do we also limit the sorts of challenge we see ahead?

 **recap**

Here is a summary of the main ideas that you can apply or bring to your own practice as a manager.

I started this chapter by saying purpose and values matter to become a brilliant business strategist. Mike Pedler, an expert in action learning, lists the main values that need to apply:[21]

- Start from ignorance. 'Not knowing' is a very powerful place to begin.

- Honesty about yourself. Who are you kidding? If it is other people, it will not last. If it is yourself, you are in real trouble.

- Have positive intent towards others.

- Do good in the world.

References

[1] A view put forward by economist Milton Friedman.

[2] http://www.ft.com/cms/s/0/6c356446-20bb-11e5-ab0f-6bb9974f25d0.html#axzz3oMeKb5Jp [accessed: 12 October 2015].

[3] http://www.ge.com/about-us/building [accessed: 10 July 2015].

[4] http://www.ey.com/GL/en/Issues/Business-environment/building-a-better-working-world-the-power-of-purpose

[5] http://www.ey.com/GL/en/Services/Advisory/EY-announcing-an-institute-for-purpose

[6] It still gets used in brochures and speeches.

[7] Gentry, W.A., Cullen, K.L. and Altman, D.G. (2013) 'The Irony of Integrity: A Study of the Character Strengths of Leader', White Paper. Center for Creative Leadership. Available from: www.ccl.org [accessed: 17 July 2015].

[8] One for the fans of the 'strategy is all about winning' school of thought?

[9] Compiled from the author's own contacts, plus http://www.jnj .com/about-jnj/jnj-credo [accessed: 3 August 2015].

[10] Look up the term 'critical management studies' if you want to know more about this aspect.

[11] http://revolv.com/static-index.html [accessed: 18 July 2015].

[12] Organization of the Petroleum Exporting Countries, headquartered in Vienna, Austria.

[13] Waitrose is part of the John Lewis Group, a partnership business owned by its employees.

[14] Mintzberg, H. (2009) *Managing*. Harlow: FT Prentice Hall, p. 14.

[15] This is driven, as always, by need.

[16] If, bit by bit, every plank, sail, rope and component of a ship is replaced with a new one, is the end result still the same ship?

[17] Revans, R.W. (1982) *The origins and growth of action learning*. Bromley, UK: Chartwell-Bratt, p. 712.

[18] Quoted in Pedler, M. (2008) *Action Learning for Managers*. Farnham: Gower, p. 5.

[19] http://www.actionlearningassociates.co.uk/actionlearning.php [accessed: 11 July 2015].

[20] Mintzberg, H., Ahlstrand, B. and Lampel, J. (1998) *Strategy Safari: Your Complete Guide Through the Wilds of Strategic Management*. Harlow: FT Prentice Hall, pp. 15–17.

[21] Pedler, M. (2011) 'The State of the Art', *Action Learning in Practice*. Farnham: Gower.

CHAPTER 9

How to break the rules of strategy

Be the change you want to see in the world.

Mahatma Gandhi

How this chapter will help you

Is strategy fit for purpose in the 21st century? Are the old rules of strategy now out of date? Systems thinking offers a different and more holistic way of looking at old views of strategy.

Introduction

At the start of the book, I offered three pieces of advice on how to be a brilliant business strategist. These are principles that work both for the organisation and the individual, so, to remind you of what they were:

- **Awareness:** because you cannot change something you have not noticed.
- **Imagination:** be ready to abandon your old maps and look at the world around you from a fresh and different perspective.
- **Positive intent:** you must be a role model.

The ideas, theories and models featured so far are like a set of rules for how to play the game of strategy in business. Without doubt, they *have* shaped how our organisations function and how we talk to each other about how they should be in the future. Although rules are important, they are also products of the past – right for their time. When you join an organisation and start learning the ropes of that particular business culture, you are taking on board a whole set of unspoken assumptions about how those things should work. The rules of strategy have all shared one enormous underlying assumption – that you and the world you operate in are separate from each other.

If you want to break the rules of strategy, you are going to have to challenge this.

looking at things from a different point of view is not easy

Looking at things from a different point of view is not easy, however. People generally prefer evolution to revolution, so it is very difficult to change the rules of business, especially when those rules look like they are producing great results. Until, that is, the old theories do not seem to resolve the new problems you face. But by then you risk it being too late. You also risk using the same logic to get out of the problem that got you into it.

 'The major problems in the world are the result of the difference between how nature works and the way people think.'

Gregory Bateson

This quote from renowned thinker Gregory Bateson has a very important point to make, but I think we often misunderstand it.

The alternative view of strategy in this chapter acknowledges and accepts that our way of thinking has, indeed, got us where we are and recognises that it is holding us back, but suggests another way out of the mess. I want to sum this up in three statements:

1 An organisation is a system, in an ecosystem.
2 Human systems function with hidden dynamics.
3 Differences between you and your environment are of your own making.

To begin with, I want to tell you what I meant by 'strategy is ecology' at the start of the book.

1 An organisation is a system, in an ecosystem

Here is a challenge for you, as a brilliant business strategist in the modern world:

---

brilliant question

How could you invent a strategy that would make all further reinvention of strategy unnecessary?

Easy? Or does it make your head spin? It turns out that this is pretty much the way that the process of evolution in nature works. Despite our human interest in change, nature rather likes it when things stay the same. The evolutionary process is very eco-

evolution has no end goal

nomical and small changes are intended to preserve the big picture. Conflict at one level may be harmony at another.

Evolution has no end goal; it is not trying to 'get' anywhere. Living systems best maintain themselves in balance (life goes on) only by retaining their ability to adapt to change.[1] Sound like a paradox? Business strategy contains a strong echo of this.

brilliant tip

The next time you attend a strategic planning session, or an awayday, see if you can get the group to identify the assumptions *behind* the mission and purpose of the business. What must be true for these to be right?

Then take the list and get people to step back from it. Ask 'what must be true for *those* things to be right?'

Let us look at some examples. When you travel to high altitude, have you noticed that you easily get out of breath? The air is thinner and your body reacts to get the oxygen. You do not have to think to activate this, your body retains the ability as automatic. If you stay up there long enough, your body acclimatises and gradually your breathing returns to normal, even when you exercise. The interesting thing is that your body will not unlearn the ability to get out breath. Evolution would run out of steam if we could make that sort of change ourselves or if we could pass our own acclimatised state directly to our kids. There are orders of change in biology. Your genes equip you with the ability to make changes, but you do not possess the ability to code any learning or talent into your DNA.

Now switch to business. As a strategist, you want your organisation to have a similar ability to change when its environment does – but you would be foolish to want to lose this underlying ability to change. In a company, this deeper flexibility can reside in the knowledge and experience of a small number of key administrators (department heads, executive PAs, functional heads, etc.). These old hands keep things running during the status quo, but have great reservoirs of experience to help adapt or innovate during a crisis. Let us look at what happens when strategic initiatives or external consultants fail to see the connection. Given a restructuring or cost-cutting exercise, they will naturally remove this layer of experience (after all, knowledge can be codified in other people's job descriptions, right?). If this is redistributed or, worse, outsourced, the business system has lost forever some potential resilience.

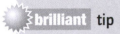 **tip**

Ecology is the study of resilience in systems.

Traditionally, the point of strategy has been to keep a single organisation in operation. Our individualistic culture permits us to do this at (almost) any cost, but this can mean pushing our costs elsewhere into the system. For a long time, that hardly mattered because the system contained seemingly abundant resources. We could see no constraints and we have enjoyed many of the benefits in our standards of living.

A system in an ecosystem

Being part of an ecosystem means being part of a balance forever. When you think of an ecosystem, probably you think of rain forests, coral reefs and deserts; habitats where all sorts of life interacts with its physical and biological environment. Within limits, an ecosystem is quite capable of sustaining itself – and it is those limits that define it (Figure 9.1).

A house is a home not because of the bricks and mortar, but because of our relationship to the space and to the people who live there. Those people are our family not just because

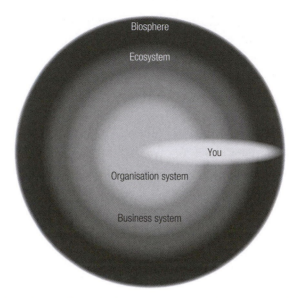

Figure 9.1 The relationship between you and the whole environment; the boundaries between every level are open

of their DNA or birth certificates, but because of the web of meaningful connections between them. By the same logic, what makes a business a business are not just balance sheets, office buildings and products but the complex and dynamic networks generated between every element of the system. In strategy, the word ecosystem gets used in two ways:

- **as metaphor:** metaphor explains one thing in terms of another and is a useful device for strategists as well as poets.[2] In fact, humans have always taken examples from nature to express something fresh and new about their own world. Calling a business an ecosystem is a useful shortcut to communicate an underlying message.

- **as paradigm:** we really *are* in an ecosystem – it is not only a metaphor. Paradigm means your worldview, and it contains everything you can normally take for granted. Paradigms are big and stable. They are a bit like tectonic plates and they shift only very occasionally. When they do, it can be big news. The farthest edge of our ecological paradigm is the biosphere. As in other complex fields such as neuroscience, we have made incredible progress in our understanding of ecology in recent years – and there is much more still to discover.

An organisation is what it is *because* it is connected to everything else in its environment.

The fate of the business ecosystem is linked to every other system. Any action, plan or strategy that damages or depletes its own context will be toxic.

 **questions**

How can you keep your business environment in balance with the survival of your organisation? Where does the accountability stop?

What would a company in tune with its environment look like? Below is an example of a manufacturing firm that is moving from one paradigm to another.

 **example**

Mission Zero at Interface Inc.

Interface Inc. is an American company that manufactures and sells carpet tiles. The firm was founded by Ray Anderson in 1973. For 21 years it followed the standard model of business growth and success in North America, using all the classic strategies of positioning to resource and finance its growth. Carpet tile production is a highly polluting process that uses enormous amounts of water and petrochemical processes. In 1994, in response to interest raised by a customer on the environmental impact of its business practice, Anderson set up a task force to look into this. He was then asked to give a kick-off speech ▷

to his team about why this mattered and what was his environmental vision. He realised he did not have one; he had never given it a thought.

It was then that he read *The Ecology of Commerce,* written by Paul Hawken in 1993. A central message of the book was that the linear *take-make-waste* business model of US industry was promoting the kind of economic activity that ends up degrading the environment it needs to maintain it. It was 'the death of birth', a line from a poem by Gary Snyder. The second message from Hawken was that those same business institutions were the *only* ones with the power, wealth and creativity to change things. This was, Anderson said, his 'spear in the chest' moment and it changed everything because it was actually a message of hope. Anderson set Interface, by then a billion-dollar business, on a course towards becoming first a sustainable business – with zero environmental impact – to eventually being a restorative one (making a net contribution to the environment).

The process evolved in the company through asking practical but holistic questions. They began with eliminating waste, which they defined as *any* cost incurred that does not produce value for the customer. Value was not defined only in economic terms. It included aesthetics as well as utility. Zero-waste went beyond reducing scrap and landfill to the elimination of *anything* that could not be got right first time. Progress was measured in dollars, so the bottom line was an important indicator and resource efficiency took over every operational and planning aspect of the business, challenging the team with new questions that gradually drew their attention outward to the relationship of the business with the environment. This was what Ray Anderson had been looking to change: to move from a linear, fossil-fuel-dependent growth pattern to a cyclical, renewable model. They now look for productivity in resources, not labour. Above all, their new technology has to be benign with the biosphere – in tune with nature, where there is no waste.

The ambition is not modest and was summed up in Anderson's (vision statement) for his company:

To be the first company that, by its deeds, shows the entire industrial world what sustainability is in all its dimensions: people, process, product, place and profits – by 2020 – and in doing so we will become restorative through the power of influence.)[3]

As part of this vision, in 2006 Interface set itself a milestone target, called Mission Zero, which is the company's promise 'to eliminate any negative impact Interface has on the environment by 2020'. Goals include sourcing 100 per cent of its electricity from renewable sources by 2020 and, by 2014, it had achieved 45 per cent (4 of its 7 manufacturing plants are now at 100 per cent). Waste to landfill fell from 5.5 million kg in 1996 to 0.86 million by 2012 and its product life cycle has been completely redesigned and rethought. Innovations have included finding ways of making the same products from fewer resources and the idea of leasing carpet tiles rather than selling them. 2020 will see a new milestone being set, as a further challenge to Interface employees as a next step.

Ray Anderson died in 2011, leaving a legacy and a mission to become a fully sustainable example to other global and international businesses.

Did you notice that Interface is using something like an action learning process internally? The founder's challenge to the organisation was 'How can we . . .?' addressing a wicked problem with no obvious answer. The company has experienced a seismic shift in thinking through answering it and 'How can we . . .?' has remained a rallying cry to action as they move to a circular business model.

⁉ brilliant question

Is it logical or sustainable in the future to think that strategy is all about winning?

What do we know about how systems work? The truth is that we are only beginning to understand how they function. And, guess what? Business and management have *not* really been at the forefront of working this out. Until recently, they have not needed to be. Business strategists have only needed to think about short-term success. For this to change, we have to switch our whole way of thinking. We

we have to switch our whole way of thinking

know that systems are non-linear – when we act in one part of an open system, it can lead to unintended and unpredictable consequences in other places at other times.

2 Human systems function with hidden dynamics

A system exists over time as complex patterns of positive and negative feedback loops and keeps stability via a balance between the two.[4] If you are interested in strategy, then you need to stop seeing a problem as *the* problem and recognise it as a symptom. It may be that strategic problems keep cropping up because you have missed the hidden dynamics at work in your organisational system. This is something I have found to be true time and again with executives and managers I work with. The way to preserve a business in the long term is by being in tune with the nature of the system of relationships at work in the environment.

The Interface example shines a light on another strategic lesson from systems thinking, which is that all human systems are subject to certain natural ordering principles. These are always at work (behind the scenes, mostly unseen and unconscious) to keep the system flowing and in balance. John Whittington is a facilitator who uses systemic constellations with individuals, teams and organisations who are snagged by systemic issues impacting their strategic intention.[5] He uses constellations to reveal these hidden organising forces in systems and to disentangle systemic dynamics. John describes the four organising principles of this:

1 **Acknowledgement:** every system is the best explanation of itself.

   Every constellation and truly systemic intervention starts with the creation of a 3D map of what is, as it is, without judgement on ideas of right or wrong. This must also be every strategist's starting point – agreeing that this is how it is – which is different to agreeing that this is right or wrong. When you can stand in the truth of what is, without moving to change too quickly, you open surprising new routes to what could be, in alignment with the natural ordering forces in the system.

2 **Time:** who and what was first in the system has precedence over who and what follows.

When this principle is ignored or violated, it entangles people and slows the system down. For example, when a new CEO joins a company, without respect for who served in the system before them, their leadership will be resisted or refused. When they can respect that the role they are occupying was created by all the work that was done by others and also occupied by someone else who made a contribution, then they can find their authority in role and create followership.

3 **Place:** everyone who has belonged in the system has an equal right to a safe place in it.

The deepest human need is to belong, so when the bonding that forms from working within organisational systems is not honoured on leaving, entanglements are created, which bind both those who leave and those who stay. Whoever and whatever is rejected or excluded by people will be remembered by the system until their contribution has been seen and acknowledged. Only in this way do people become free and do organisations become disentangled from their past and move into the future.

4 **Exchange:** all systems require a constant dynamic balance of give and take.

Underneath conscious methods, such as salaries and bonuses, there is a much more important balance of exchange to pay attention to. A strategic leader who wants to create flow and vitality in their organisational system will want to pay attention to creative ways of balancing what employees, business partners and others give with what they take. This must also be applied to strategy. A systemic strategic leader can ask themselves and their team 'What does our strategy give to those who work in its service?'

This is the briefest of introductions to the kind of systemic leadership that supports the flow of organisational vitality, but these underlying principles will start to reframe your thinking about truly strategic leadership.

3 Differences between you and your environment are of your own making

In a 2015 survey of 6,000 CEOs conducted in the UK by management consultants PwC,[6] only 8 per cent of respondents were categorised as 'strategist' (one of seven 'action logics' developed by David Rooke and William Torbert[7]), possessing a set of talents normally associated with building long-term strategic transformation. Figure 9.2 shows how people in the survey matched up against the five highest-order categories. Most people were placed in the two roles most associated with getting things done. Over half were 'achievers', effective in managerial roles and good at carrying out strategy, whilst a third were 'individualist', able to innovate structure and use interpersonal influence for strategic ends. But very few blended all those qualities with the ability to think on their feet and reframe the dilemmas and paradoxes that they meet.

No one in the survey was profiled in the top category – alchemist! Does that mean there are virtually no truly transformational leaders out there? Worryingly, the same survey was conducted 10 years earlier and not much had changed in results, despite the many books and articles written about leadership and strategy. What should your conclusion be from that?

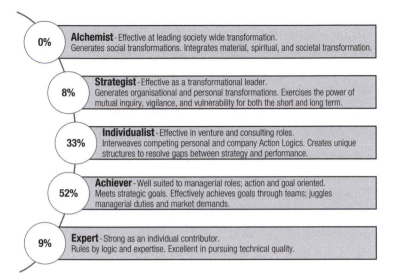

Figure 9.2 Leadership talents
Source: Extract from PricewaterhouseCoopers 2015 survey, 'The hidden talent: Ten ways to identify and retain transformational leaders'. Reproduced with permission.

 **question**

If you were in charge of a large organisation and this data was about the leaders in your company, what would you be inclined to do about it?

I hope your first reaction would be, by now, not to panic, but rather to stop and think. Prioritising the system, and not the individual organisation within it, is a huge shift to make.

Strategic decision making: an old way

How should a strategist think? How should a brilliant business strategist make their decisions? And what sort of person should they aspire to be? Until now, we have thought of decision making as a fairly rational process. Understanding organisational decision making was the life's work of the Nobel laureate economist Herbert A. Simon. In 1947 he published a book called *Administrative Behavior* and, throughout his long career, he further developed his interest in rational decision making. Simon's influence still dominates our worldview of how organisations come to decisions. In particular, two concepts stand out:

1 **Bounded rationality:** the idea that you will not know everything. People must admit that, because their information is limited, they can make rational decisions only up to a point. They have to be pragmatic. They combine the following:

   ● what they know about the situation;

   ● what they know about their own thinking limitations;

   ● how much time they have to devote to thinking before they need to act.

   Does that sound like how people talk about decision making where you work?

2 **Satisficing:** follows from this and is the apparent willingness of managers to settle for the adequate, but not optimal, solution once they have looked at enough of the alternatives available to them. Again, this is because they believe they will never have *all* the information available out there. You may see this at work when people say, often with a frustrated and stressed look on their face, 'Can't we just make the decision and move on?'

In fact, these have become part of the rules of how we do strategy. But they *only* make sense for problems in management that are:

● part of a closed system in which possible outcomes are limited (and there may actually be one right answer);

● linear and mechanistic, to be analysed, understood and controlled, and separate from what goes on in the world outside.

'Taking a linear process and drawing it as a circle doesn't make it non-linear.'

David Snowden

When you apply that thinking to an open system, you are faced with a problem; it can make matters worse. To get out of this conundrum you need to rethink your assumptions. The biggest assumptions you have to question are the ones about how you think in the first place. Managers who do this as part of their work are what Donald Schön (an American academic referred to in Chapter 5) calls **reflective practitioners.**

 **tip**

The aim of reflective practice is to cultivate being unsure.

Strategic decision making: a new way

To break the rules of strategy you also have to stretch, bend and investigate the rules of self.

Coming to terms with who you are may be the greatest strategic mission you will ever make because exploration of this is also a kind of meeting the world. There are lots of things you can do to start this development journey. Here are a few ideas.

Practise mindfulness

This has become very popular in management lately.[8] Mindfulness is a secular application of Buddhist meditation technique, but requires no prior knowledge or religious belief. Harvard professor John Kabat-Zinn has pioneered the use of this as a technique in the clinical treatment of stress and anxiety and it is proving useful in many non-clinical situations, including at work.

 **definition**

Mindfulness

Mindfulness means paying attention in a particular way; on purpose, in the present moment, and non-judgmentally.

John Kabat-Zinn[9]

You are mindful in any situation and in doing any activity (including strategy) when you are fully present and non-judgmental.

Go system-spotting

As you go about your day, start to notice systems. A visit to almost any business, organisation or social event is a way of stepping inside the boundaries of someone's system. Of course, you are part of many systems yourself: at home, at work and in your community. In fact, our family is the first system we are aware of, so its importance is tremendous – even for grown-up strategists!

Observe what is going on in each case. Can you identify where the system's boundaries are? What is inside, and what is not? What crosses between one system and another? What is each system for and what emerges from it? You may like to observe a system over time. How does a system change? What happens if you move a boundary (such as in a merger or acquisition) or when a governing rule is changed? How does the system keep its pattern? As an example, you might see whether Richard Branson's Virgin, a varied group of companies, has an underlying pattern that is systemic in nature.

brilliant tip

When you start to notice the systemic world, you can respond to change by becoming part of it. This is a non-judging and accepting attitude, but not a passive one.

Strategy is a bit like Aikido, a Japanese martial art: the flow of an attacking force is redirected in a way to leave both you and (ideally) your attacker unharmed.

> strategy is a bit like Aikido

Learn about improvisation

Good jazz musicians know something every strategist should learn: the power of 'Yes, and . . .' thinking. When you watch jazz artists improvise, no idea is ever wrong and no idea is rejected. There are no mistakes in improvisation and the point is not to get to a particular place. In strategy, once you know what the basic rules are, you can incorporate any change around you into what you are doing, accepting that this will create further change in unexpected ways. Contrast this with the 'Yes, but . . .' thinking found in many organisations, in which rigid mindsets are resistant to any information from outside that could alter the goal or objective.

 **example**

David Bowie

Now almost 70, David Robert Jones is better known as David Bowie. His complex and long career exhibits a systemic approach to strategy.

Bowie's major success as an artist began in 1969 with a solo hit single, *Space Oddity*. But, before this, he had spent years learning and perfecting the rules and rituals of performing. In common with many young people, he was in a series of failing bands and artistic projects (he also studied dance and mime artistry) in the vibrant cultural scene of the 1960s. Having made the breakthrough to mainstream during the 1970s and 1980s, he then produced a series of hit albums and singles. Every recording project appeared with its own image, persona or musical style. By all accounts Bowie has always been single-minded and strong-willed and committed to his own vision (and desire for success), but what has given him longevity has been an ability to combine his surroundings – different people, places ▶

and events – with his creative method to explore new themes. His adaption of William S. Burroughs' 'cut-up' technique to generate new ideas and lyrics is a good example of this methodical and creative approach. Bowie has consistently managed his durability by managing his availability, so that he ends each phase or stage on a high and then retires from public view.

You might conclude from all of this that David Bowie's career has been a series of contrived and commercial moves; that it could be classic strategic planning, careful product positioning and clever promotion.

On the other hand, you could also conclude that Bowie's success shows many of the hallmarks of systems thinking:

● a strong sense of purpose that connects a wide variety of projects;
● the re-entry of ideas and events into the mix and, every time an idea returns, it is transformed. His own legends and stories (heroes and villains) are recycled and any paradox created is actively embraced (and never explained);
● an ability to learn through an unfolding and emergent process;
● a recursive persona (the sum is different to the parts);
● positive feedback loops that are checked by negative ones;
● context, not content, that creates meaning. We have a relationship with the work of the artist.

David Bowie is a brand and a business as well as an individual. How self-aware do you think the brand is? How much of the brand is also the person? It would be difficult to know, of course, without asking him, though there is evidence that as a businessperson he is self-observant.

 'Self-observation is seeing everything in you and around you as if it was happening to another person.'

Anthony de Mello, spiritual teacher, writer and public speaker

Looking beyond the music, how do you rate David Bowie as a strategist? Are there lessons for management and business? BBC journalist Will Gompertz certainly saw some parallels when he wrote:

David Bowie is the Steve Jobs of rock, the Picasso of pop. He synthesises influences past and present, drops them into the Bowie Blender, and serves up something fresh and exciting. Jobs would come up with a new product, Picasso a new style; Bowie launches a new persona.[10]

In business, the longest-surviving companies are not necessarily those that have the smartest plan, come up with the best product or employ the cleverest people (these are all important), but are the ones that have the most systemic flexibility: neither dwelling in the past nor living in the future, but fully alive in the present.

 'The first thing to think about the future is to know about the present.'

Hans Rosling, Swedish Professor of International Health and renowned public speaker

The Tao of being a brilliant business strategist

The strategist's basic question is 'How can I make this better?' We are all searching for a better way. It seems to be in our nature to want to force any issue or problem to a solution. We have to *know*. And yet we struggle to find answers in our noisy, non-stop world. It eludes us.

we are all searching for a better way

This is a very focused and stressful way of being.

Systems thinking is a reminder that we are very selective in all that we see. Perhaps the question that eludes us most is 'Who am I?'

Long before our modern concept of selfhood, there have been other, much older views, such as the Tao (or Dao), which translates – roughly – into English as *the way*.[11] The Tao is an enigmatic and ancient philosophical tradition from China. One of its central ideas is seeing the world as a system of interrelating components; no part exists independently from any other. In Taoism, all opposites mutually arise from one another. The best-known book on Tao is the *Tao Te Ching*, a collection of cryptic verses by Lao-Tzu.[12] Here are its famous opening lines:

The Tao that can be told
is not the eternal Tao.[13]

This message seems mischievous. Applied to our keyword, strategy, you end up with something like 'If you think you know what strategy is, then you don't'. The true Tao of an organisation is that it is what it is, by itself, completely in tune with its environment. And you are, naturally, a part of that. What is even more baffling is the claim that you are perfect, *and* can be improved upon. But not through force. That would be like straightening water (the Tao does rather get you to hook into patterns in nature). There are many important passages in the *Tao Te Ching* for a brilliant business strategist. A lot of them are connected to leadership (the strategist who lords it over others is not a strategist at all). I think this is captured nicely in this extract:

If you don't trust the people,
you make them untrustworthy.

The Master doesn't talk, he acts.
When his work is done,
the people say, 'Amazing:
we did it, all by ourselves!'[14]

The best leaders serve by getting out of the way. They do this by trusting that their staff have the power already and their job is to make themselves available to their staff as a resource. 'How can I help? is their way of liberating their colleagues and employees through trust.

the best leaders serve by getting out of the way

brilliant tip

Your job, as a brilliant business strategist, is to nurture the space for others to act in. They already have the power to do this – you cannot give it to them. You can, however, provide the guidelines that will create the freedom for them to build the business.

Putting it all together: strategic leadership in service of . . . ?

Leadership in a system means acting in service of something that may be beyond your immediate surroundings. This goes much further than our usual definition, even when companies talk about corporate social responsibility (CSR).

To be a strategic change leader, start by acknowledging that you see the world through preconceived ideas (preconceived means they are based on past facts). Above all, begin by fully acknowledging where you are now, in the world as it *actually* is, and suspend judgement. Only then will you be able to make yourself aware of what you cannot see and what you do not know.

brilliant tip

The belief that it is the manager's job to be in control of outcomes is an illusion. The world around us is truly complex and you can only be in tune with your environment, not in control of it.

It might seem strange to close a book about strategy with a tip on letting go. After all, are managers not supposed to be

the less you have to do, the more you can achieve

masters of control? This is a paradox, for sure, but the more you are involved with the search for strategic issues and the delivery of strategic decisions in your organisation, the more you realise that the less you have to do, the more you can achieve.

 **brilliant** recap

Here is a summary of the main ideas that you can apply or bring to your own practice as a manager:

You now have *three* ways to judge a strategy:

- **Rationally and analytically:** the normal way of understanding how an industry works is by studying how individual organisations function inside it, or by studying single aspects such as marketing or finance (and do not forget, no real-life business problem is ever contained under one label). The systemic way says that you must see the whole, not the parts.

- **Morally and ethically:** corporate social responsibility (CSR) and sustainable development treat the problem as one of ethics. As long as we are morally responsible in limiting how much damage we do in economic growth and consumption, then we can preserve the current state of affairs for future generations. The best case is that it will not get any worse (or not too much worse).

- **Ecologically:** the shift is from a conquering and controlling attitude ('It is us *against* our environment') to one that is less arrogant and more dynamic ('It is us *perceiving* our environment'). Lots of organisations have, in the past, become very good at the first one. The new challenge is to become much better at perceiving our environment by becoming aware of, and tuned in to, the ecosystem.

Many organisations are not fully conscious of how they create their strategy. Because CEOs are paid to know these things, this causes them terrible problems! But the truth is that a lot of what an organisation does to keep itself going is done unconsciously and unawares.

The CEO's real job is to create the space and the potential for a strategy to emerge from the collective purpose of everyone involved in the organisation. This is quite a skill and many of the ideas in this book will help you identify the kind of data that shows you what may not normally be visible in your immediate surroundings.

But for *that*, you need a shift in your thinking.

brilliant question

Think about your definition of strategic leadership. Has it changed as a result of what you have read?

References

[1] This is also called homeostasis.

[2] Business examples include machine, computer, organism, DNA, etc.

[3] http://www.interfaceglobal.com/company/mission-vision.aspx [accessed: 22 July 2015].

[4] Also called homeostasis.

[5] Whittington, J. (2016) *Systemic Coaching and Constellations*. 2nd Ed. London: Kogan Page.

[6] PricewaterhouseCoopers (2015) 'The hidden talent: Ten ways to identify and retain transformational leaders'.

[7] Rooke, D. and Torbert, W. (2005) 'Seven Transformations of Leadership', *Harvard Business Review* 83(4), pp. 66–76.

[8] I prefer the word *awareness,* as it carries a bit less baggage.

[9] Kabat-Zinn, J. (1994) *Wherever You Go, There You Are.* New York: Hyperion.

[10] Gompertz, W. (2013) 'The business of David Bowie', BBC News. Available from: http://www.bbc.co.uk/news/entertainment-arts-21861596 [accessed: 1 August 2015].

[11] This could be understood as path or route, but it also works as 'how things are'.

[12] The Tao Te Ching dates from about the 6th century BC, but almost certainly there was no person named Lao-Tzu. It is a collection of 81 verses.

[13] Mitchell, S. (2006) *Tao Te Ching: A New English Version.* New York: HarperCollins, p. 1.

[14] Mitchell, S. (2006) *Tao Te Ching: A New English Version.* New York: HarperCollins, verse 17.

Epilogue

I think it's wrong that only one company makes the game Monopoly.

Steven Wright[1]

This is the end of a journey through the varied landscapes of strategy. Now would be a good time to reflect, so look back at the five statements on strategy in the introduction to the book. Have your impressions changed? Which intrigues you more to read further?

 **tip**

Strategy is about moving forward to the future – but this process *always* starts (and only happens) in the present.

Pick up a strategy book from 10 or 20 years ago, and the chances are that you will still recognise much of its contents. Knowledge of the conventional theories of strategy certainly helps, but blind adherence to any particular doctrine – particularly if its assumptions are not in tune with how things are – is a limit on what you can do in the future, when it may be too late to respond. We are playing for high stakes.

> we are playing for high stakes

A good strategy should be the most natural thing in the world. It ought not to be a struggle to set a course of action – and, as long as you are standing honestly in the right place, with the right attitude, with no baggage and with the right skills to lead with vision and humility, there is a lot that can be done.

 **example**

Raw milk, straight from the cow[2]

The Richardson family have been dairy farmers in the Worcestershire countryside south of Birmingham for three generations. In recent years, fluctuations in the price of wholesale milk have meant that the current generation, Rob Richardson and Heather Couper, found they cannot fund investment in new equipment or long-term improvements for a large herd. At first, they looked at producing and selling premium products of their own and experimented with beef, pork and free-range eggs. But then they spotted an unmet market need – raw milk. Pasteurised makes up 99.99 per cent of all milk production in England, so demand for the raw product is small. This, however, suited their ambitions for a reduced herd size and Straight from the Cow was born in January 2015. Selling direct, its customers are buying mostly for the health benefits (e.g. lactose intolerance, eczema, asthma, IBS) or as part of a diet prescribed by their faith. Heather agreed to be interviewed for this book.

Q **What market research did you do?**

A Honestly, we did very little. We knew we needed to do something quite quickly and had minimal funds to invest. We had looked at making ice cream and cheese with our milk, but the cost of the equipment was too great. We did read copious amounts of literature about various case studies into raw milk, both science-based and from farmers who had chosen a similar route.

Q **What is your vision for this business?**

A I hope that we will continue to grow our customer base. We still sell the majority of our milk as wholesale and lose money on every litre. The smaller proportion of milk we sell raw helps to stem the impact of this. We have tried several avenues of advertising and marketing. Some have been positive and others a waste of time and money. I hope we will learn as time goes by what works for us and how best to spread the word about raw milk amongst the correct groups of people. We also hope to grow our farm meat and egg business, too, as selling a wider range of products does seem to draw more customers to our farm.

Q **What would you say has been your strategy so far? Is this something you planned or did it emerge as you went along?**

A We have travelled some avenues that may not have been particularly fruitful, but we are building a business as a family and finding new strengths within our team. We are learning as we go what works and what has not and trying to work more efficiently and making the best of the avenues that have been rewarding. I suppose we have slightly been winging it, but we do have a lot of family discussion and we do make decisions based on what direction we, as a family, want to move the business.

Q **What is your passion? What (apart from the 50 cows needing milking) gets you up in the morning?**

A Easy. I love where I have grown up and the life I have lived. It's been hard, sometimes soul destroying when you work seven days a week, not unheard of to work through the night, and there is still no money to take a wage. I love walking around a field at 5 am when no one else is up and it's just me and the cows. I love to go to bed physically exhausted because I've worked so hard and my feet hurt. I love what farming has made me as a person. I appreciate where food comes from and the sweat and tears (literally) that have gone into providing it. I love the heritage that is linked to the farm and I hope I will be able to pass on a profitable and beautiful farm to future generations. The thought of selling my childhood home and a business/home my ancestors worked so hard for fills me with horror.

There are two things I like about this story. First, the importance given to being productive and innovative whilst maintaining the sustainable limits on the resources available; they do not want to be the next big thing – and they do not need to be. Next, there is the selection of a strategic direction that maintains a real connection to place and stays in tune with the values of the family system by preserving the underlying pattern from one generation to the next.

> some of the best companies to work for often feel like family

It is, perhaps, no accident that some of the best companies to work for often feel like family.

References

[1] Quoted in Jarski, R. (Ed) (2004) *The Funniest Thing You Never Said*. London: Ebury Press, p. 336.

[2] www.straightfromthecow.co.uk

What did you think of this book?

We're really keen to hear from you about this book, so that we can make our publishing even better.

Please log on to the following website and leave us your feedback.

It will only take a few minutes and your thoughts are invaluable to us.

www.pearsoned.co.uk/bookfeedback

Further reading

Thanks very much for your book. I shall waste no time in reading it.

Benjamin Franklin

There are thousands of books and articles that will inform your thinking about strategy (remember, a brilliant business strategist needs inspiration from many sources, so look beyond business and management as well). The suggestions below will help you dig a bit deeper into some of the topics and themes in this book. They include some textbooks that cover more ground than there has been space for here, as well as some of the better-known titles by influential university professors. I have avoided, with one exception, books by leaders and CEOs reminiscing on their careers – these tend to be of their time and most do not travel well.

Chapter 1

HBR's 10 Must Reads on Strategy (2011). Boston: Harvard Business Review Press (*Harvard Business Review* is worth seeking out for major statements on mainstream strategic thinking).

Mintzberg, H., Ahlstrand, B. and Lampel, J., (2008) *Strategy Safari: Your Complete Guide Through the Wilds of Strategic Management.* 2nd Ed. Harlow: FT Prentice Hall.

Greene, R. (2007) *The 33 Strategies Of War.* London: Profile Books.

Chapter 2

Johnson, G., Scholes, K. and Whittington, R. (2013) *Exploring Strategy Text & Cases*, 10th Ed. Harlow: Pearson.

Moore, J. (2001) *Writers on Strategy and Strategic Management: Theory and Practice at Enterprise, Corporate, Business and Functional Levels*. 2nd Ed. London: Penguin Books.

Chapter 3

Kiechel, W. (2010) *Lords of Strategy: The Secret Intellectual History of the New Corporate World: The Secret History of the New Corporate World*. Boston: Harvard Business Review Press.

Carter, C., Clegg, S. and Kornberger, M. (2008) *A Very Short, Fairly Interesting and Reasonably Cheap Book about Studying Strategy*. London: Sage.

Chapter 4

Porter, M. (2004) *Competitive Strategy: Techniques for Analyzing Industries and Competitors*. New Ed. New York: Free Press.

Hamel, G. and Prahalad, C.K. (1996) *Competing for the Future*. Boston: Harvard Business Review Press.

Chapter 5

Christensen, C. (2013), *The Innovator's Dilemma: When New Technologies Cause Great Firms to Fail (Management of Innovation and Change)*. Reprint Ed. Boston: Harvard Business Review Press.

Govindarajan, V. and Trimble, C. (2010) *The Other Side of Innovation: Solving the Execution Challenge*. Boston: Harvard Business Review Press.

Chapter 6

Brown, S., Bessant, J. and Lamming, R. (2011) *Strategic Operations Management*, 3rd Ed. London: Routledge.

Armstrong, M. (2011) *Armstrong's Handbook of Strategic Human Resource Management*. 5th Ed. London: Kogan Page.

Kotler, P. and Chernev, A. (2012) *Strategic Marketing Management*. 7th Ed. Chicago: Cerebellum Press.

Chapter 7

Heath, C. and Heath, D. (2011) *Switch: How to Change Things When Change is Hard*. London: Random House.

Tushman, M. and O'Reilly, C. (1997) *Winning Through Innovation: A Practical Guide to Leading Organizational Change and Renewal*. Boston: Harvard Business Press.

Chapter 8

Reiman, J. (2013) *The Story of Purpose: The Path to Creating a Brighter Brand, a Greater Company, and a Lasting Legacy*. London: John Wiley & Sons.

De Wit, R. and Meyer, R. (2014) *Strategy Synthesis: Resolving Strategy Paradoxes to Create Competitive Advantage*. 4th Ed. Connecticut: Thomson Learning.

Pedler, M. (2008) *Action Learning for Managers*. Farnham: Gower Publishing.

Chapter 9

Anderson, R. (1998) *Mid-course Correction: Towards a Sustainable Enterprise*. Atlanta: Peregrinzilla Press.

Autry, J. and Mitchell, S. (1998) *Real Power: Business Lessons from the Tao Te Ching.* London: Nicolas Brealey.

Bateson, G. (1972) *Steps to an Ecology of Mind.* New Ed. (2000) Chicago: University of Chicago Press (not for the faint-hearted, a very difficult but rewarding read).

Twenty prominent strategists

Many of the names on this list are practitioner academics. A few are wholly academics, whilst one or two are wholly CEOs and business leaders or entrepreneurs. What and who influences strategy is part of the problem everyone seems to face in finding a good definition. One depressing observation is that they are nearly all men. Strategy, for some reason, has yet to discover that half the world's population are women! It may also be fairly accused of defining itself in a period of First World versus Third World economics that does not exist in our time. Nevertheless, everyone on this list rewards study, even if (perhaps especially *when*) you do not agree with them. Whether the next generation of strategic thinkers will be drawn from other walks of life and from the new economies remains to be seen, but strategy would be a healthier subject if there were greater diversity.

- **Andrews, Kenneth R.** (1916–2005) was a Harvard Business School professor. He helped devise the SWOT matrix and the external/internal approach to corporate strategy. He was a member of an influential group of thinkers at Harvard after the Second World War who advocated strategy as a structured process.

- **Ansoff, Igor** (1918–2002) was a Russian-American pioneer of corporate strategy by objectives; he is known by MBA students worldwide for his matrix of generic strategies. But Ansoff had a more varied and considered career than this. He was a thought leader in many areas of corporate planning and never forgot the importance of people in the management mix.

- **Chandler, Alfred** (1918–2007) was an influential American economist who wrote about the relation between strategy and structure, the importance of visible middle management in implementing planning and corporate decentralisation in business transformation.

- **Christensen, Clayton** (1952–) is another Harvard business professor. He has studied how large organisations become vulnerable to 'disruptive innovation' in an industry when new technologies arise. His best-known book is *The Innovator's Dilemma*, published in 1997.

- **Drucker, Peter** (1909–2005) – few names are more illustrious (or quotable, as you may have gathered) than Drucker's. When it comes to the subject of mapping what management is, how the modern corporation should be led and what the role of knowledge is in the setting of direction and strategy, he has influenced just about every other writer on this list.

- **Fayol, Henri** (1841–1925) was a French mining engineer who, at the turn of the 20th century, employed a keen eye for meticulous observation, chronicling good management practice in his industry. His 6 functions and 14 principles of management were published in English only several decades after his death, but became core to the creation of our modern definition of the management function.

- **Hamel, Gary** (1954–) is an American management consultant, speaker and academic who is best known for developing and promoting the idea of core competences, alongside C.K. Prahalad. He is now also well-known for his interests in the future of management thinking and innovation in strategic transformation.

- **Hampden-Turner, Charles** (1934–) is an influential British philosopher and management thinker, whose interests over a long career have included the role of dilemma and paradox in innovation – an important topic for strategists – as well as the social impact and obligations of management and business.

- **Handy, Charles** (1932–) is an Irish philosopher, management thinker and prolific author who has written about how organisations can be structured in new ways to meet the changing needs of the business environment and how people (including himself) can find renewal and reinvention during their careers.

- **Henderson, Bruce** (1915–1992) founded the Boston Consulting Group in 1963 and was one of the first systematically to apply years of experience gained in industry, much of it at Westinghouse, to the study of variables in management decision making. In particular, Henderson pioneered the careful analysis of competitive forces in business growth.

- **Machiavelli, Niccolò** (1469–1527) was a Florentine diplomat and philosopher (amongst many other interests) during the Renaissance. He is best remembered today for his treatise on leadership, power and politics, *The Prince*, written in 1513. In the context of the time, it was a shrewd analysis of authority and rule in the midst of competitive forces, but it covers a range of aspects of ruling and is not quite the manifesto for bad behaviour that many people think.

- **Meadows, Donella (Dana)** (1941–2001) was an American environmental scientist and writer. She studied biophysics and was one of the first to research the consequences of long-term economic activity and other trends on systems and their capacity to renew themselves. Her best-known book, *Limits to Growth,* was published in 1973 and her 1999 essay on various ways of intervention in a system, *Leverage Points: Places to Intervene in a System* is now considered a classic.

● **Mintzberg, Henry** (1939–) is a Canadian academic, speaker and author. He is a professor of management and strategy with a knack for bridging the divide between what strategists are told they should do and what they actually do. Critical of some of the more static schools of thought, Mintzberg's entertaining style has helped put strategy back into open circulation as an emerging topic.

● **Musk, Elon** (1971–) is a naturalised US citizen and the man who set up online payment company PayPal. He now has a string of businesses exploring commerce, transport, electric powertrain systems, solar power generation and space exploration. He is an influencer and a visionary who has the funds to pursue his ideas. It will be interesting to see whether this turns him into a strategist in the eyes of others in years to come.

● **Ohmae, Kenichi** (1943–) is a scientist, academic and management consultant who is known for his work explaining Japanese working practices and long-range planning mindset to a western audience, developing our understanding of the nature of globalisation in business and commerce amongst conglomerate enterprises.

● **Porter, Michael** (1947–) has been the cause of many books and debates on strategy, either by those who agree with and build on his work, or those who position themselves somewhere else by comparison. A Harvard professor and author of many books on competitive strategy, he is the mainstream voice in the application of economic theory to strategy.

- **Prahalad, C.K.** (1941–2010) was a University of Michigan professor, perhaps most associated with the development of the core competences approach to resource-based strategy with Gary Hamel, but he also made a significant contribution to management practice and wealth development in his native India.

- **Sloan, Alfred** (1875–1966) is one of those names now enshrined as a seminal figure in the story of management and corporate strategy. He is credited with developing General Motors during the Great Depression and Second World War into a multinational giant through rational, meticulous production planning and marketing.

- **Stacey, Ralph** (1942–) was born in South Africa and is a professor at the University of Hertfordshire in the UK. Through his early work, he was a key voice in the inclusion of complexity and systems theory into management and planning of organisational strategy, whilst now he has shifted to the study of complex responsive systems amongst human beings.

- **Taylor, Frederick W.** (1856–1915) is of the same generation as Sloan and is remembered for defining what we now usually call scientific management, which combines precise study of time and motion, scientific selection and training, training and development to task and the division of tasks for industrial productivity. This is also known as Taylorism and remains influential, albeit under new names.

Index

Page numbers in *italic* denote figures and tables.

Do you want your people to be the very best at what they do?

Talk to us about how we can help.

As the world's leading learning company, we know a lot about what your people need in order to be better at what they do.

Whatever subject or skills you've got in mind (from presenting or persuasion to coaching or communication skills), and at whatever level (from new-starters through to top executives) we can help you deliver tried-and-tested, essential learning straight to your workforce – whatever they need, whenever they need it and wherever they are.

Talk to us today about how we can:

- Complement and support your existing learning and development programmes
- Enhance and augment your people's learning experience
- Match your needs to the best of our content
- Customise, brand and change it to make a better fit
- Deliver cost-effective, great value learning content that's proven to work.

Contact us today:
corporate.enquiries@pearson.com